50 GREAT MOMENTS in AUSTRALIAN CRICKET

Published by Affirm Press in 2021
28 Thistlethwaite Street, South Melbourne,
Boon Wurrung Country, VIC 3205.
affirmpress.com.au
10 9 8 7 6 5 4 3 2 1

A catalogue record for this
book is available from the
National Library of Australia

NATIONAL LIBRARY OF AUSTRALIA

Title: 50 Great Moments in Australian Cricket / Dan Liebke, author
ISBN: 9781922626073 (flexibound)

Cover and internal design by Karen Wallis, Taloula Press
Typeset in Garamond 10 / 15pt
Printed in China by C&C Offset Printing Co., Ltd.

50 GREAT MOMENTS in AUSTRALIAN CRICKET

DAN LIEBKE

CONTENTS

THE SPIRIT OF CRICKET

THE EVOLUTION OF CRICKET

THE TACTICS OF CRICKET

THE NUMBERS OF CRICKET

THE COMEDY OF CRICKET

INTRODUCTION

Cricket is a gem of a sport.

Like any half-decent gem, cricket can dazzle us with its brilliance, holding our attention for far longer than should be possible. It's a precious sport, priceless to its devotees.

Cricket also sparkles from every angle you choose to examine it. Although, it is, of course, best observed in the sunlight of a cloudless day, where its luminance shines brightest.

In addition, cricket, like many gems, may contain flaws, yet be beautiful despite them – or perhaps because of them.

Cricket is *not*, however, one of the myriad valuables hoarded in Smaug the Dragon's caves of Erebor or Scrooge McDuck's personal money bins. (This is despite the pair's ongoing tussle for top spot in the Forbes Fictional 15, the list of the richest fictional characters as calculated by the *Forbes* business magazine.) Cricket is not a gem in that sense. It's important to know the limits of your metaphors. To keep a tight rein on your literary conceits. Otherwise, you run the risk of wasting the time of an otherwise serious financial periodical by ranking the relative wealth of imaginary ducks and lizards.

So we'll be keeping our 'cricket is a gem' analogy under control from here on in this introduction, and restrict it to one final point of similarity.

That point is that cricket, like most gems, has multiple facets. And that's what this book will explore as we roll the sport around in our fingers, squinting at it through our goofy-looking jeweller's microscope monocle thing. As we examine cricket's various facets, we'll try to determine what makes the sport so special.

We'll focus primarily on events of the last fifty years, and limit our gaze mostly to matches that feature Australia. Australian cricket is a subset of cricket. But it's a *big* subset. The Australian men played the first Test, the first One Day International and the first T20 International. The Australian women also played the first women's Test and the first women's ODI. They had to settle for the second women's T20 International (England and New Zealand pushed in ahead of them). But the Australian women have since compensated for that snub by crushing every team that dares cross their path in the format. So examining cricket primarily through a baggy green lens (some kind of woollen emerald, perhaps?) provides us with plenty of moments that define the sport. (And if a few of those moments have only tenuous links to Australia, then so be it. Why should our exploration of what makes cricket such a great sport be hindered by the shameful unAustralianness of other cricketing nations?)

The fifty great moments in the history of cricket in this book illustrate all the fascinating facets of the sport. The skill of cricket. The Laws and the Spirit of Cricket. The evolution and the tactics. The numbers and the comedy. All these aspects will be covered.

We'll start with a gem. A diamond, to be precise. Or, at least, a man with a diamond stud in his ear. It's 1993, and he's about to thrill everybody watching with a moment of unparalleled skill.

THE SKILLS OF CRICKET

SHANE WARNE

BOWLS MIKE GATTING

Balls of the Century

THE MOMENT:

In 1993, with his first delivery in Ashes cricket, Australian leg-spinner Shane Warne bowls 'the Ball of the Century' to dismiss Mike Gatting

We've all seen the footage. Shane Warne comes in to bowl his first ball in Ashes cricket. The delivery fizzes out of his hand, swerving through the air towards leg stump. The ball touches down outside leg stump, where it bounces and turns with improbable sharpness. It snaps back past the bat and into the off stump. Ian Healy jumps in the air in delight. On commentary, Richie Benaud divulges the simplified version of what just took place: 'And he's done it.' Celebrations ensue.

It's the most famous delivery in the history of cricket. The ball of the century.

The delivery didn't take place until the second day of the Test. England had won the toss and chosen to field first, which limited Warne's bowling opportunities on the first day. Even at his peak, Warne rarely took wickets while Australia was batting. But after Australia were knocked over for 289 early on the second day, it was time for Warne to show what he could do. It took until England had reached 1/80, however, before captain Allan Border threw the ball to him.

There was curiosity about Warne in England at the time, but little of it had to do with his bowling. Yes, he'd performed well against New Zealand in his most recent series, taking 17 wickets in three Tests. But overall, he'd taken 31 wickets in eleven Tests, at an average of 30.80. Nothing to get excited about on that front. Leg-spin bowling was always an exotic conversation piece, for sure. But had you noticed that this Warne character was blond? With an earring! Playing an Ashes Test! Can you imagine such a thing?

That confounding first ball to Gatting refocused attention on his bowling. Even more so when Warne continued to tear through England that northern summer, taking 34 wickets at 25.79, with Australia securing a 4–1 series victory.

When the ball to Gatting was later anointed as the Ball of the Century, it was justifiable. We were already 93 per cent done with the 20th century. Enough had been seen to make the claim. But the number of claimants for the ball of the *21st* century is really rather extraordinary, given that there remain eighty-odd years to go.

There's Ryan Harris's ball to Alastair Cook in the 2013/14 Ashes. Australia needed ten wickets to reclaim the Ashes for the first time since 2007. So Harris summoned a first ball of the innings that seamed in, then swung away to clip the bail of the off stump. Cook was later knighted. Despite this sensational delivery, Harris was not.

Presumably, this ball was also too good for the Queen, causing her to dub and miss.

Four years later, Mitchell Starc put forth his own ball of the century candidate. In Perth he let fly with a 143-kilometre-per-hour ball angled down leg side. Not a problem for the batter. At least, not until it hit a crack and jagged back 42 centimetres – *twice* the width of the stumps – to smash James Vince's understandably exposed off peg.

There are others. Plenty of others. In 2006, Pakistan's Mohammad Asif pre-empted Starc's ball *without* WACA crack assistance to cartwheel VVS Laxman's middle stump. Against left-handed Indian opener Sadagoppan Ramesh in 2001, Muttiah Muralitharan came around the wicket to deliver the off-spin equivalent to Warne's Gatting ball. Then did the same trick from over the wicket a year later to undo England's Mark Butcher.

All these balls were dubbed 'the Ball of the Century' by excitable commentators, journalists and/or fans. As indeed were many others, including several from Warne himself.

Perhaps the best candidate came from fellow Australian leg-spinner Amanda-Jade Wellington. In the 2017 Women's Ashes, she pulled out a near perfect replica of Warne's original to bowl Tammy Beaumont. It swerved past the leg stump line, ripped back, beat the outside edge of the bat, crashed into the off stump and everything. There was even a jubilant Healy (Alyssa) in the background celebrating the dismissal.

Wellington's ball of the century contender is a standout not only because of its similarity to Warne's, but because it's another leg break. Leg-spin is the most difficult form of bowling, so balls of the century from a leg-spinner score bonus points.

However, despite the quality of all these deliveries, the issue is clear. There are far more balls of the century than one might traditionally expect in a mere couple of decades of 21st-century international cricket.

This is a problem.

There is a psychological technique designed to stoke addictive behaviour. That technique is called 'intermittent reinforcement'. It works on the idea that if you want somebody to behave in a certain way, you should not reward them for that behaviour *every* time. Instead, rewarding them only occasionally and unpredictably turns out to be far more effective.

The success of this technique has been observed by the kinds of scientists who like to tease rats with random morsels of food. Closer to the real world, poker machines deal in pure intermittent reinforcement. Hence their addictiveness for some people.

Do you find cricket gripping and difficult to turn your attention away from? That's probably because the game has its own form of intermittent reinforcement.

As a rule, runs tick over steadily, but wickets? They tend to fall at irregular intervals. Heck, even the worst tailenders in history (think Chris Martin, Glenn McGrath, an out-of-form Joe Burns) are more likely to survive any single delivery than lose their wicket to it. It's what makes the final innings of a tight Test match so gripping. The drip-drip-drip of the runs required for victory coming down, combined with the erratic nature of when a wicket might fall. Even in a far-fetched run chase, with the wickets likely to fall before the target is reached, you can never know exactly *when* those wickets will come.

This is intermittent reinforcement at its best. Your reward for following cricket on a ball-by-ball basis is the rush of dopamine whenever a particular ball delivers a wicket. And if the fall of a wicket is like a poker machine paying off, then the fall of a wicket to a Ball of the Century is like a Mega Jackpot paying off. An outsized reward for our actions.

But if it happens *too* often, then we undercut the entire intermittence that is at the heart of intermittent reinforcement. Unintermittent reinforcement (to use the scientific term I've just invented) is nowhere near as effective as its *un*unintermittent counterpart.

Yes, it takes an exceptional sport to have balls of the century that occur more often than our standard understanding of chronology permits. But for balls of the century to continue to impress us, they need to stop happening quite so often.

NEXT:

What happens when wickets are so unintermittent that three of them fall in a row? On a bowler's birthday? Plus, rabbit jaws!

PETER SIDDLE

TAKES A HAT-TRICK ON HIS BIRTHDAY

Hat-tricks

THE MOMENT:

On the first day of the 2010/11 Ashes, Peter Siddle celebrates his birthday by taking a Test hat-trick

For the first twenty-five years of his life, Peter Siddle celebrated his birthday in a normal fashion. He'd open presents, feign enthusiasm about them, then eat cake until he threw up.

On his twenty-sixth birthday, however, Siddle got greedy. Like a precocious primary schooler, he took his birthday wish and wished for more wishes. Then he crammed in as many sub-wishes as he could.

'I wish I could play my first home Ashes Test in front of a packed Gabba crowd, and help bowl England out on the first day for only 260, and take a six-wicket haul, and also take a hat-trick, and maybe even have Ricky give me a new BMX – a red one with flash racing stripes.'

And because it was his birthday, somehow it all came true. While England won the toss and chose to bat, they never got away from Australia. In the first innings, anyway. In the second innings, England finished on 1/517d, a trademark 'getting away' innings. (This second innings took place *after* Siddle's birthday, and hence was beyond the purview of his all-powerful wish.)

In the first innings, England reached 4/197 in the final session of Siddle's birthday, when the newly minted 26-year-old began his hat-trick.

It started with Alastair Cook playing forward at a ball outside off stump. The edge flew to a delighted Shane Watson at first slip.

One ball later, 5/197 became 6/197. A 142-kmh full ball from Siddle proved too fast for wicketkeeper Matt Prior, knocking over his middle stump.

Stuart Broad, at the very peak of his Malfoyness, arrived at the crease to face the hat-trick ball. Three years later, Broad would react to a rampaging Mitchell Johnson by spending eight minutes adjusting a sight screen. He would then be hilariously bowled first ball. In 2010, however, Broad spent no time on sightscreen adjustment. Nor was he bowled first ball, in hilarious fashion or otherwise. Instead, he was LBW, with another full ball from Siddle zeroing in at the base of the stumps.

Siddle leapt and pirouetted in midair to appeal, but Aleem Dar had already raised his finger. After a brief discussion with non-striker Ian Bell, Broad momentarily dimmed the Australian celebrations. He punched fist to forearm and reviewed the decision.

Of course, every decision that Broad reviews is destined to not go his way. The ball-tracking therefore denied him a reprieve. And the celebrations of Siddle's birthday hat-trick echoed anew around the Gabba.

The day ended with England all out for 260 and Australia 0/25 in reply. A satisfied Brisbane crowd saluted the young fast bowler's feat as he rode back to the team hotel on his wicked new Mongoose BMX.

(Things went less well for Australia during the rest of the series, as they were thrashed 3–1 by an indomitable England team. For the rest of the series, there was only one other Australian cricketer who played a Test on his birthday. That was captain Ricky Ponting, who celebrated his thirty-sixth birthday in Perth by overseeing his side's only win. The selectors' refusal to acknowledge the power of birthday wishes was, in retrospect, a critical factor in the home Ashes loss.)

Siddle's birthday hat-trick was the defining moment of his career. This was despite the best efforts of certain television commentators to later talk up his tendency to eat bananas. The banana talk was tiresome, because the hat-trick was always far more interesting than a fondness for a run-of-the-mill grocery item. That's because hat-tricks are innately compelling. If, as theorised, one of the keys to cricket's appeal is the intermittent reinforcement of wickets falling, a hat-trick is the temporary suspension of that intermittency.

If a 'ball of the century' is a single moment of improbable quality, a hat-trick generally dials down the quality, only to compensate in quantity. (Although, if somebody wants to take a hat-trick with three balls of the century some day, be my guest. At that point, we'll completely give up on the whole idea of balls of the century appearing once per hundred years.)

To follow up one wicket with another wicket first ball to the new batter is far-fetched enough. (Let's not get too bogged down with Merv Hughes–style hat-tricks over multiple overs and multiple innings. These 'trick hat-tricks' are for advanced users only.) Even though a batter is most vulnerable when they're first at the crease, it's still asking a lot to take their wicket at the first possible opportunity. To then follow up that unlikely feat by doing it again is an idea that should be too implausible to contemplate. Especially since the notion is so powerful that everybody – from fielding side to new batter to crowd to umpire to banana-obsessed commentator – is aware of the significance of the moment, and how preposterous it is to expect it to unfold as hoped for.

But it's that very unreasonable-ness that makes a hat-trick, when it happens, so thrilling to behold. It's a magician pulling a rabbit from a hat — and then yanking open the rabbit's jaws to pull out another hat. Inside of which is another rabbit.

Other sports have hat-tricks of various kinds, but none are quite as rare as the cricketing version. This makes hat-tricks a next-level example of intermittent reinforcement. You have to watch several overs of cricket to have a reasonable chance of seeing a wicket fall. But you have to watch fifty or so Tests to have a reasonable chance of seeing a hat-trick. It's a reward for the more seasoned cricket watcher, one who dedicates years to the sport.

This kind of intermittent rein-forcement, at both the micro and macro levels, makes cricket more and more riveting the more you watch it. If you were designing a sport to grow more addictive, the more you become involved with it, you honestly couldn't wish for anything better.

Not even a flash BMX from Ricky Ponting.

NEXT:

Hat-tricks from bowlers are improbable. The equivalent for fielders are catches that, for lack of superior alliteration, we deem to be 'classic'. Plus, satirical wartime novels!

JOHN DYSON

GRABS AN OUTFIELD CATCH

Classic Catches

THE MOMENT:

In the second Test of the summer of
1981/82, West Indies tailender Sylvester
Clarke lofts Australian off-spinner Bruce
Yardley into the outfield, where John
Dyson takes an eye-popping leaping catch

'That's some catch,' observes Yossarian in Joseph Heller's satirical wartime classic *Catch-22*.

'It's the best there is,' comes the reply from Doc Daneeka.

Of course, the characters in the book are referring to the titular Catch-22, a paradoxical law built on self-contradiction. However, they could just as easily be referring to John Dyson's stunning goalkeeper grab. Assuming, that is, that we overlook the fact that Yossarian and Daneeka were both (a) stationed on an island off the coast of Italy during World War 2, forty-odd years before Dyson took his catch and (b) fictional.

Dyson's grab was part of a striking spell of bowling from Bruce Yardley. The off-spinner took the final seven West Indies wickets as the visitors fell from 3/179 to 255 all out.

The Dyson catch gave Yardley his fifth wicket, and it's difficult to imagine a five-wicket haul being brought up in more dramatic fashion. A lofted slog from Clarke to wide long on had Dyson skipping backwards with ever-increasing urgency. With each hop back, he reassessed the shot's trajectory. Only at the last moment did Dyson realise that to be in the correct position to take the catch would take more than mere hopping and skipping. Which meant he had to jump.

As jumps went, it was an almighty backwards Fosbury flop of a thing, with both arms outstretched and straining for the ball. Miraculously, Dyson intercepted the ball with his right hand. He clung to it with the unbreakable grip of the vacuum cleaner with which he shares his name, even as he crashed to the ground. Clarke was out. Yardley had his fifth. And Dyson had taken a screamer.

Having batted at three in the first innings, Dyson then opened the batting in Australia's second. From there, he guided the home side to the security of a draw with a six-hour 127 not out, his highest Test score. Yet as fine as that century was, it was still overshadowed by his incredible catch. Not just in this match, but over his entire career.

The catch instantly became the archetype for outfield catches: the standard against which all others were measured. A Dyson catch became shorthand for a particular brand of outfielding excellence. If it wasn't the best catch ever, then it would always be in the conversation.

One of the difficulties of declaring *any* catch the best is that catches come in all shapes and forms. Each of those shapely forms shows off different skills. And those skills are appreciated by different kinds of fans.

Does it even make sense to compare a brilliant grab in the slips with a running and diving take in the deep? The first will be defined by reflexes and reaction time (notable exception: Mark Taylor juggling a catch with his feet). The second by speed over the ground and judgement of the ball's flight (and, these days, willingness to get a teammate involved). Sure, they're both catches, but is it reasonable to declare one better than the other?

Well, yes. Yes it is. Especially if you want to take part in a Classic Catches competition.

Admittedly, in modern times there's little incentive to take part in such a contest. Classic Catches were once beloved parts of every summer. Then broadcasters discovered they could charge people to send them text messages. And Classic Catches segments devolved into fried chicken–based telemarketing schemes. Ones with only a passing interest in the recognition of spectacular snares.

A Classic Catches segment in the modern format is flawed from its initial conceit. (Even if we ignore the purported reward of gorging down fast food on a weekly, sponsor-subsidised basis.) A modern Classic Catches contest isn't won by an entrant voting for the *best* catch. Instead, they win it by voting for the catch with the most votes.

That kind of circular illogic should have been stamped out the moment the format was developed. Instead, it was somehow allowed to slip through. And once that was allowed to slide, the entire structure of modern Classic Catches decomposed.

Heck, one summer in the dying days of Channel Nine's coverage of the game, they even included a Faf du Plessis catch that he took off a no ball. It's old-fashioned, perhaps, to think of a 'classic catch' as being one that's actually caused the batter's dismissal. But if anything was a harbinger of Nine's imminent demise as the official broadcaster of the game in Australia, it was madness such as this. What was next? Adding run-out attempts to the segment? Return throws to the keeper? Particularly high-intensity fielding drills? Thankfully, Nine's time was cut short before we could find out.

It was all a far cry from the good old days of the 1980s, when Classic Catches was a summer-long journey of ranking excellence. During that decade, Classic Catches candidates were logged throughout the cricket season. In the summer's last few weeks, they were whittled down to a top seven. Then that supreme septet of snares was screened over and over in those final weeks to ensure as many television viewers got to see them as possible. Finally, those viewers who wanted to enter the competition filled out a form attempting to rank those seven catches in the same order as Nine's commentators (a 1 in 5040 chance) and mailed it in.

That was the classic form of Classic Catches. The proper form. With nary a KFC Maxi Popcorn Chicken Combo to be seen.

Catches that made the final list became enshrined in the public consciousness. Through both repetition and contemplation of their relative merits. It's why the Dyson catch – the winner of the 1981/82 season of Classic Catches – is still remembered so fondly forty years later.

Any television broadcaster who returned the original 'rank the seven best catches of the summer' form of Classic Catches to screens would no doubt be rewarded handsomely with more engaged viewers. But would they be rewarded handsomely enough to convince television station bean-counters to pry the format away from the ephemeral but lucrative 'SMS your vote for this week's best catch (or catch-like moment)'? That's the question.

Maybe the only way to convince broadcasters to get rid of the SMS poll format of Classic Catches is by having them run an SMS poll on the matter.

A classic catch-22 for Classic Catches.

Yossarian was right. That's some catch.

NEXT:

Balls of the century, hat-tricks and classic catches are all rare. But the rarest record of them all belongs to a batter. Plus, unkillable alien hobgoblins!

CHARLES BANNERMAN SETS THE OLDEST RECORD

Individual Performances

THE MOMENT:

In the very first Test match, Charles Bannerman of Australia scores 165 out of a team total of 245, a contribution of 67.3 per cent, a record that has never been broken

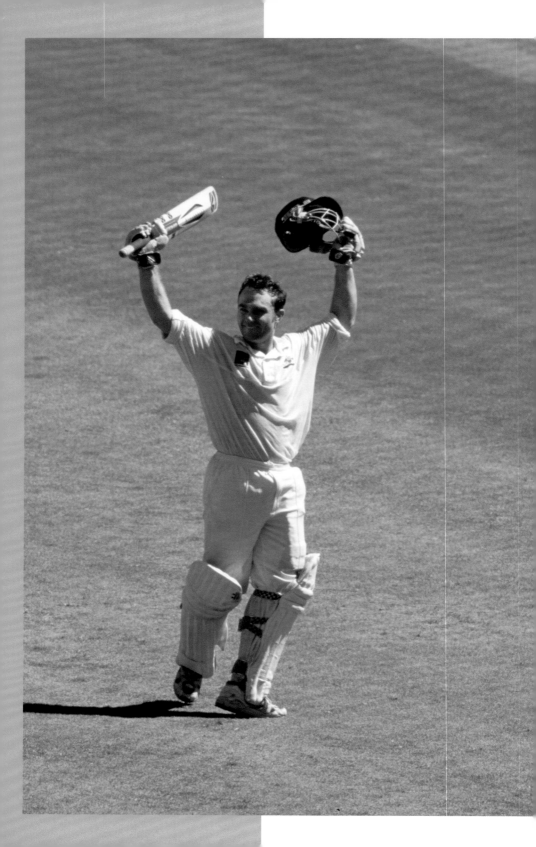

There's no 'i' in team. There is, however, one in cricket. Along with two 'c's, a 'k', an 'r' and 1982's favourite unkillable alien hobgoblin, E.T.

But as tempting as it might be to divert immediately into a discussion of the xenobiology and agoraphobia of a beloved cinematic extra-terrestrial, that's not what this book is about. Or, if it is, there will be plenty of time for it later. Instead, let's divert into a discussion about cricket's unique relationship between individuality and teamwork.

Cricket is, ostensibly, a team sport. There are eleven players on a team, all competing against the opposition's eleven players. In this it's much like football, field hockey or eleven-a-side tennis.

Yet within the team structure of cricket, individualism runs rampant. We've all seen partnerships in various fields of human endeavour where one of the pair was substantially less talented than the other. Think Simon and Garfunkel. Or Hall and Oates. Or the Olsen twins.

These kind of unbalanced partnerships also exist in cricket, particularly when batting. But one of the great things about cricket is that such grotesque skill mismatches can be circumvented. Indeed, such is the structure of the sport that it's possible for a sufficiently skilled individual batter

to score an *unlimited* number of runs. This is true regardless of the talent, or lack thereof, of their batting partner.

As long as the non-striker can stay in their crease and then stroll to the other end of the pitch on the final ball of each over, the talented batter can get the job done. Furthermore, if that same batter is more talented than *every* other member of the team, that's no problem. They can open the batting and control the strike for the whole innings, reducing a team sport to an individual showcase.

Of course, such complete batting dominance by an individual has never been seen; it remains a purely abstract possibility. But one of the best things about cricket is that the closest anybody has ever come to achieving this feat came in the first Test match ever played.

Charles Bannerman attained several records in that Test, many of which by definition cannot be broken. He faced the first ball in Test cricket, scored the first run and wore the first silly cap. He also scored the first fifty and the first century.

But the most impressive Bannerman record is one that could have been broken in the 144 years since, yet somehow hasn't been: he scored the highest proportion of his side's runs in a completed team innings – which is to say, one in which the batting side was bowled out. Bannerman made 165 not out before retiring hurt thanks to a broken finger (to quote E.T., 'Ouch!'). His runs represented 67.3 per cent of Australia's total of 245.

The standard for individual batting dominance of this team sport had been set. It has never been surpassed. (At least, not in men's cricket. In women's Tests, Enid Blakewell of England scored 112 not out in a team innings of 164 in 1979, pipping Bannerman by less than one per cent.)

There is, it should be acknowledged, some minor naysaying about the Bannerman record. Some statisticians claim that the retired-hurtedness meant that Australia were in fact only ever nine wickets down. The innings therefore wasn't a 'completed' one.

If one excludes Bannerman, the record in men's Tests falls to Australian opener Michael Slater. In Sydney in 1999, he made 123 in a completed team innings of 184, a proportion of 66.8 per cent. However, Slater was almost certainly run out for 35 during this innings. He was only given not out because the television replays failed to find a clean angle of the stumps being broken while his bat was out of the crease. This was despite the fact that even the most primitive use of split-screen technology would have shown him several inches out of his ground. Still, since the victims of this pedantic third-umpiring were England, who in the 1990s were always getting into such comical misadventures, nobody made too much of a fuss.

The point is, if we have to have some pedantic controversy over who the legitimate record-holder is, let's give it to Bannerman. At least he can claim to never once having irritated us with his television commentary.

But it's not just batting in which an individual can dominate a cricket match. A bowler can similarly monopolise a match. The initial impulse here is to turn to Jim Laker, who in 1956 took nineteen wickets in a Test match: nine in the first innings and ten in the second. Or Anil Kumble, who replicated the ten-wickets-in-an-innings feat in 1999.

But both those bowlers relied on the assistance of teammates to take catches. A truer measure of bowling individualism would only count wickets that were taken bowled, caught and bowled, or hit wicket. (Leg before wicket dismissals are a grey area, given their dependence on the opinion of the umpire and/or ball-tracking computer programmer. Timed out is even murkier, as it would have to be proven that the tardy batter was reticent to arrive at the crease for fear of facing the bowler.)

With those individualistic restrictions in place, Johnny Briggs from England is our bowling Bannerman. In the second Test against South Africa in Cape Town in 1889, he took 8/11 from 14.2 overs in South Africa's first innings of 43. Every wicket he took was bowled. When South Africa made 47 in the second innings, he took 7/17 off 19.1 overs, six bowled and one LBW. Briggs was, it must be assumed, a stump-to-stump bowler.

Briggs took fourteen of the possible twenty wickets bowled, the most individualistic form of dismissal. And the 70 per cent proportion is eerily close to the Bannerman equivalent in batting.

Yet while cricket allows for such individual dominance, it can also be played in the purer team form. In 1963/64, South Africa made 302 all out in the first innings of the first Test against New Zealand. The highest individual score was 44. The rest of the scores were 24, 22, 31, 30, 40, 30, 27, 7, 24 and 2 not out. It was the most consistent completed batting innings in Test history. Heck, even extras contributed 21.

The corresponding most shared bowling performance in a Test again came in a match between South Africa and New Zealand. This time in South Africa's second innings of the first Test of the 2005/06 series. New Zealand used seven bowlers, each of whom took either one or two wickets. (If we extend our scorecard gaze beyond Tests, we find an Ireland v India women's ODI in 2006. In that match, India used eight bowlers, seven of whom took a wicket, with the other taking two. Oh, and there was also a run-out. A team performance for the ages.)

Within these broad extremes of individualism and team performances lies the entirety of cricket. And faithfully guarding the limits of cricket individualism is Bannerman, with his 'innings of the sesquicentenary'. That's how you do it, bowlers.

NEXT:

A more recent example of individual heroics compensating for the shortfalls of the rest of the team. Twice in one summer! Plus, Turbo Boost buttons!

BEN STOKES
STEALS THE HEADINGLEY TEST

Miracle Innings

THE MOMENT:

In the Headingley Test of 2019, Ben Stokes scores an unbeaten century in the final innings to secure a miraculous one-wicket win for England and keep the Ashes alive

In the very first match of the 2019 World Cup, Ben Stokes began his magic summer by top-scoring in England's first innings of 8/311. His innings of 89 off 79 balls wasn't, however, the moment that stuck in the memory. That was a valuable innings that ensured England reached a defensible total. But the moment that had all cricket fans around the world gaping in awe was the one-handed, Dysonian catch that Stokes took on the boundary.

The commentary of Nasser Hussain reflected most people's reactions. 'No way,' he said. 'No. No way. You cannot do that, Ben Stokes.'

But Hussain was wrong. Ben Stokes *could* do that. And as the summer went on, he unveiled a whole heap of other remarkable things that he could do. All of which most sane people would have responded to with an emphatic 'no way'.

Stokes's 'no way' moments before 2019 had generally been of a negative ilk. On the cricket field, he had always seemed fuelled by a combination of Red Bull, inexplicable rage and imminent heatstroke. He did everything with a furious intensity and energy that often seemed to undercut his attempts to play the best cricket he could.

His first Test wicket was taken away from him when, in striving for extra pace, he overstepped and no-balled. He punched a locker in the West Indies after being dismissed for a duck. (He'd been playing in the West Indies at the time . . . it wasn't like he flew over there from Lord's or somewhere to punch that one specific locker.)

He was enraged to be given out for obstructing the field when he parried away a throw at the stumps from Mitchell Starc while out of his ground. And, of all his pre-2019 'no way' cricketing moments, he'd most infamously continued to charge in and bowl deliveries that Carlos Brathwaite then deposited in the crowd to snatch victory in the 2016 World T20 Final.

(There was also, of course, an off-field 'you cannot do that' moment for Stokes when he was involved in a late-night Bristol street brawl. This incident saw him arrested and charged with affray. While later found not guilty by a jury, the incident still cost him the opportunity to take part in the 2017/18 Ashes.)

In between these 'no way' downsides, Stokes had many triumphs. He established himself as one of the finest all-rounders in world cricket. He hit mind-boggling centuries and double-centuries. He took unplayable five-wicket hauls. He snared catches that most cricketers would not even process as chances.

Yet in the summer of 2019 he would surpass all those previous triumphs, with the 'no way'-est pair of 'no way' innings any batter could hope for.

First, there was the World Cup final. Since their ramshackle effort in the 2015 World Cup, England had built the best ODI team in the world. They'd established a fearless attacking batting mindset that left every other team in their wake. (Not only *in* their wake, but lying awake as they tried to work out how to combat it.)

Yet England had never won a World Cup. And the final was at home, at Lord's, in front of a crowd torn between expectation and ingrained pessimism. The pressure threatened to become too much.

Chasing New Zealand's 8/241, a total far short of the 300-plus targets they'd effortlessly run down over and over in the previous few years, England stumbled to 3/71 in the twentieth over. That was when Stokes arrived at the crease.

They were soon 4/86 when captain Eoin Morgan fell. A run-a-ball 59 from Jos Buttler got England within striking distance of the total. But New Zealand were still favourites.

And yet Stokes hung in there. Run by run, he whittled down the target, charging between the wickets like a madman, hitting the occasional four or six to keep in touch. With three balls remaining, he managed both a four *and* a six in one ball. His desperate dive for the crease for a second run as the fielder's throw came in saw the ball deflect off his bat and go to the boundary for a bonus four runs – making six in total.

Off the final two balls, attempted twos became singles and run-outs. It left the World Cup final tied in a fashion that could only be described as breathtaking.

Fittingly, then, Stokes took a breath. Then came out and did it again. He batted in the Super Over and scored enough runs to ensure another tie. And with that came a World Cup win on the basis of a boundary countback.

No way, Ben Stokes.

As far as second-best innings by an individual in a summer go, Stokes's World Cup knock is surely the best. (Read that previous sentence again if you have to. I promise it makes sense.) Because a little over a month later, Stokes came up with something even more impossible.

England were bowled out for 67 in the first innings of the third Test in reply to Australia's 179. The visitors then scored 246 in their second innings to set England a target of 359 for victory. (Stokes took 3/56 from 24.2 overs in Australia's second innings, bowling more overs and taking more wickets than any of his teammates.)

As with most fourth-innings targets in excess of 300, it always felt like it was only a matter of time before the wickets fell. Sure, England might whittle down some runs in the meantime. But they couldn't possibly do so fast enough to reach the target before the inevitable ten wickets fell. The wickets would fall intermittently, but they *would* fall.

This turned out to be 90 per cent true. When Stuart Broad, the ninth wicket, was dismissed, England were still 73 runs short of their target. Stokes was still in the middle, but he'd spent most of his innings focused on survival, looking to build partnerships.

Now, with nothing to lose, Stokes pressed the big red Turbo Boost button and went for the win. He reverse-swept Nathan Lyon for six. He flicked Pat Cummins over the keeper for six. He played perfectly normal cricket shots that also went for six.

Between the thunderous sixes, Stokes stole delicately placed twos and singles to minimise the strike for Jack Leach. It drove Australian captain Tim Paine to distraction. It drove Australian coach Justin Langer to the brink of kicking over a dressing-room garbage bin. And it drove the Headingley supporters into a frenzy.

Somewhere in there, Stokes brought up a century he didn't bother to acknowledge, so intent was he on the match target.

And then, after both a near-miss run-out and a near-miss LBW with only two runs needed for the win, Stokes crashed a cut shot to the boundary. It ensured a stunning victory for England that kept the Ashes alive. (For a fortnight, anyway.)

It was an emphatic 'no way' to the 'no way'-sayers. Because in this particular 'yes way' summer, there were no limits to what Ben Stokes could do.

NEXT:

Not all all-rounders are created equal. Some are at a whole other level. Plus, Highlander swordplay!

ELLYSE PERRY

SCORES A DOUBLE-CENTURY

All-Rounders

THE MOMENT:

During the Women's Ashes Test of 2017, Ellyse Perry scores an unbeaten double-century, the highest score in the history of Women's Ashes

It's one of the highlights of Ellyse Perry's Australian career. She uses quick footwork to get to the ball, timing her shot with tremendous power. It's driven hard, but with perfect precision, lofted over the outstretched gloves of the keeper. The ball flies all the way, landing a few metres in front of the cheering crowd.

If you're finding such a cricket shot difficult to recall – or even imagine (a drive that's gone over the keeper's head?) – that's hardly surprising. Because I'm not referring to a cricket shot at all. I'm referring to a goal that Perry scored at the 2011 FIFA Women's World Cup. A near perfect left-footed blow from outside the penalty box that curled into the top corner of the net. The goal allowed Australia to go in at half-time 2–1 down. Perhaps even with a chance of causing a quarter-final upset against one of the tournament favourites, Sweden. (2011 FIFA Women's World Cup spoiler: they didn't.)

In a sense, it's hardly surprising that an elite cricket all-rounder would be so athletically gifted they could excel at the highest level in a completely different sport. We also see it in Perry's male parallel as Australia's finest cricketing all-rounder. That's Keith Miller, who averaged 36.97 with the bat and 22.97 with the ball. He took 170 wickets and scored just shy of 3000 runs in his 55-Test career from 1946 to 1956.

But before his cricketing heroics, Miller had, like Perry, been a successful footballer. Miller's code of choice was Australian Rules football, where he played for St Kilda. The Saints had signed Miller as a nineteen-year-old. This was after they saw him negate veteran full-forward and future Hall of Famer Bob Pratt in a VFA match. Miller played a total of fifty matches for St Kilda. In that time, he showed the full extent of his all-rounderness by switching from full back to the forward line after his first season. Thirty-two matches into his VFL career, he then switched from the forward line to the frontline, heading off to fly Mosquito fighter-bombers in World War 2. After the war, he returned to the Australian football fields.

But, as with Perry, the lure of cricket proved too strong for Miller. Despite representing Victoria in 1946, the excitable comic book writers who seemingly wrote the story of Miller's life decided to switch his Australian Rules career for a role in the Australian cricket side.

Needless to say, Miller soon proved himself an all-rounder without peer. He was an integral part of Bradman's 1948 Invincibles side. He was also one of only three men whose names appear on both the batting and bowling honour boards in the Lord's visitors' dressing-room. (The others were Garfield Sobers and Vinoo Mankad, both of whom we'll get to later.) Miller was also the retrospectively calculated number-one-ranked ICC all-rounder for almost his entire career. (We'll get to rankings later too.)

Ellyse Perry hasn't been the number-one-ranked ICC all-rounder for her *entire* career. (Although she was close enough that the ICC named her as T20 and ODI player of the decade in late 2020. And, of course, as the women's cricketer of the decade.)

Until 2015, Perry was a bowling all-rounder, who was handy with the bat. Then the excitable comic book writers who wrote the story of *her* life decided she could have a lot more fun adventures if it wasn't always about bowling heroics. She'd already bowled her side to a 2013 World Cup victory on one leg. Where else was there to go in terms of dramatics? It was time that she also dominate the sport while batting too.

And so she did. Because, why not?

The transformation in Perry's batting reached its peak in the 2017 Test between Australia and England. She smashed 213 not out during the match, the highest score in the history of Women's Ashes.

She batted at number four in the absence of regular captain Meg Lanning. From there, Perry watched as the side slumped to 5/168 in reply to England's first-innings total of 280 all out. Undeterred, she combined with the lower order in back-to-back century partnerships. First, she batted with Alyssa Healy to achieve near-parity with England. Then, with Tahlia McGrath, to establish a dominant lead. Finally, she pushed her own score past the double-century mark.

Although, not without some confusion.

When Laura Marsh tossed the ball up, with Perry on 194, she used quick footwork to get to the ball, timing her shot with tremendous power. It was hit hard, but with perfect precision, lofted over the outstretched hands of the fielder at deep midwicket. The ball flew all the way, landing a few metres in front of the cheering crowd.

Except, not quite.

Despite the excitement of the fans and Perry's ensuing acknowledgement of the landmark, the ball hadn't *quite* cleared the boundary. The third umpire confirmed it was only four. Perry had to wait until the next over to bring up her actual double-century, a landmark so monumental she celebrated it twice. (Although, slightly sheepishly the second time around.)

Perry's achievements in both cricket and soccer are unparalleled in modern Australian sport. (She may well be conquering sports faster than we can invent them. This could become an unsustainable situation at some point.) They certainly dwarf the most recent attempt by a man to represent at an elite level in both cricket and a football code.

That man was Andrew 'Joey' Johns, a rugby league Immortal. (Much like in the movie *Highlander*, rugby league players are deemed to be Immortals of the game if it's proven that they can be killed only by severing their heads with a sword.)

In a piece of 2007 marketing reasoning that has perhaps aged poorly, the New South Wales cricket side decided that the silly new T20 cricket format would only be interesting if it were spiced up by the presence of a rugby league player in the side. And so Johns was shoehorned into the New South Wales side, where he bowled one over and batted at number eleven.

While theoretically a piece of fun, the marketing gimmick cost New South Wales any chance of making the final. With thirteen needed from the final over, captain Simon Katich refused to risk giving the strike to Johns. That seemed fair enough, given the bowler was Ryan Harris, a man capable of dismissing and/or injuring players with far greater batting skill than the ludicrously out-of-his-depth halfback.

Johns played one other match for New South Wales in the tournament. He scored 9 from 10 deliveries. The experiment was then abandoned.

Still, hell of a rugby league player, though.

NEXT:

You don't need the transcendent skill of a Perry or a Miller to impact a match. Even a part-time bowler of limited skill can make a contribution. Plus, mind thorns!

ALLAN BORDER
SPINS AUSTRALIA TO VICTORY

Part-time Bowlers

THE MOMENT:

At the SCG in early 1989, Australian captain Allan Border takes eleven wickets in the match to upset the mighty West Indies side

For as long as Allan Border had been in the Australian side, he had been a thorn in the West Indies side. For the entire 1980s, Clive Lloyd's and Viv Richards's men had run rampant over the cricketing world. Their endless supply of terrifying fast bowlers destroyed all who dared oppose them.

All, that is, except Border, a stubborn, stubbled terrier of a cricketer who refused to back down from the most fearsome attack in Test history.

Throughout the 1980s, of all the batters who played more than a handful of Tests against the West Indies, not a single one was able to average more than 50. The closest was Border, who averaged 46.41 against the men from the Caribbean. He achieved that average while scoring 1439 runs from the nineteen Tests he played against them. Nobody else played more Tests against the West Indies than Border during the 1980s. And only England's Graham Gooch scored more runs against them in that time (1589 at 41.81).

In 1984, Allan Border produced one of the great individual Test cricket performances. In a Test match in Port of Spain, the capital of Trinidad and Tobago, he scored 98 not out and 100 not out to ensure Australia escaped with a draw. This was the match that stamped Allan Border as one of the great batters of his era.

What he wasn't, though, was a great bowler.

Which was what made the events of the fourth Test against the West Indies in the summer of 1988/89 so astonishing.

Viv Richards's side had already taken an unbeatable lead in the five-match Test series. They'd won in Brisbane, Perth and Adelaide by nine wickets, 169 runs and 89 runs respectively. Any form of Australian resistance had been swatted away. (The Brisbane defeat would be Australia's last at the Gabba for 32 years, until India won the Border–Gavaskar series there in 2020/21.) In among the Test victories, the West Indies had also crushed the ODI tri-series, defeating Australia in the finals.

But the SCG was different. In a decade of Australian misery against the West Indies, the Sydney Cricket Ground was the one ground at which the home side had held their own.

In fact, better than held their own. In 1981/82, they'd secured a draw. In 1984/85, they'd won by an innings, as spinners Bob Holland and Murray Bennett bedevilled an all-star batting line-up consisting of Gordon Greenidge, Desmond Haynes, Richie Richardson, Larry

ALLAN BORDER SPINS AUSTRALIA TO VICTORY

Gomes, Viv Richards, Clive Lloyd and Jeff Dujon. The SCG, with its spin-friendly surface, offered Australia its best chance each series to defeat the West Indies.

Yet that still doesn't quite explain what Border accomplished in 1989. In accordance with tradition, Australia had augmented their spin attack for the Test. They gave leg-spinner (and future chief selectorial scourge of both Mark Taylor and Steve Waugh) Trevor Hohns a first cap. He played alongside established off-spinner Peter Taylor.

The West Indies, begrudgingly, also added a specialist spinner to their attack. Roger Harper replaced Patrick Patterson in the starting eleven, to give them a grand total of one (1) spin bowler.

But when Viv Richards won the toss and his top order cruised to 1/144, there was little sign of what would happen next. Yes, the pitch was dry and turning, even on day one, which had allowed Peter Taylor to take the sole wicket to fall to that point.

However, Border's gentle left-arm orthodox spin was nothing special. Before this Test, he'd taken a grand total of sixteen Test wickets in 99 Tests. Yet he dismissed Richie Richardson with a long hop, then a

couple of overs later Carl Hooper with essentially the same ball.

Viv Richards was next, 'caught' at short leg from a ball that seemed to miss his bat. Hohns then got Haynes, for the tongue-twisting fun of it, before Border continued his rampage. The Australian captain snaffled the next four wickets as the West Indies were all out for 224.

Border finished with figures of 7/46 from 26 overs. In his hundredth Test, he'd completely flipped the script on the West Indies. For so long the West Indies bowlers had struggled to curtail him with the bat. Now it was their batters' turn to have no answers to Border with the ball.

He continued in the second innings, taking a further four wickets to finish with match figures of 11/96. Only Greenidge and Walsh avoided losing their wicket to Border, as his gentle turners from around the wicket proved inexplicably unplayable.

Australia went on to win the Test by seven wickets. Border hit the winning runs, but for the only time in his long career it was his bowling that had proved the difference.

It's not as if the pitch was an unplayable turner, either, as the records of the other spinners showed. Peter Taylor finished with three for the Test and Hohns four. For the West

Indies, both Harper and Hooper went wicketless. Richards, understudying the 'reluctant part-time finger-spinning skipper' role, took a sole wicket in each innings. Instead, it was Malcolm Marshall who dominated for the West Indies. The great fast bowler cared not one iota about the notion of a spinners' wicket, taking six wickets for the Test.

Border's eleven-wicket haul remains an unexplainable anomaly. You can understand a part-timer jagging a wicket or two here and there. But eleven? It makes no sense. Paradoxically, that lack of sense may have been the key to Border's success. After getting lucky with his first couple of wickets, perhaps he got into the heads of the West Indies batters.

Each wicket Border took with no logical explanation must have had the next batter looking for the key to the mystery. A misplaced focus on Border's accumulating wickets prevented them from focusing on the basics of batting. The basics that ordinarily served them so well.

The irony is that if Border had been a better bowler, there would have been a more plausible explanation for him taking wickets. That, in turn, would have allowed the batters to play him on his merits and deny him further wickets. Instead, as the batters searched for danger that wasn't there, they inadvertently summoned that very danger into existence.

Granted, this doesn't make much sense. A bowler taking wickets because they so rarely take wickets? That's a paradox to test any cricket fan's mind. Fittingly so, because what Border's eleven wickets show is the extent to which cricket is not merely a game that tests physical skills. It also tests the mental strength required to apply those skills.

Border had been a thorn in the West Indies' side ever since he'd been in the Australian side. Rarely had that led to a victory (just two in nineteen matches before this one). However, at the SCG in 1989, he was a thorn in their mind. And that worked much better.

NEXT:

Being a mentally strong cricketer is vital. Especially when your physical body has been broken. Plus, South African dental hygiene!

GRAEME SMITH

BATS WITH A BROKEN HAND

Heroism

THE MOMENT:

With fifty balls remaining in the third Test of the
Australia–South Africa series in 2009, Proteas
captain Graeme Smith walks out to bat at
number eleven with a broken hand

For a few seconds it looked like it was over. After dropping a sharp caught-and-bowled chance two balls earlier, seamer Andrew McDonald jagged one in to Dale Steyn. The ball thumped into his pad, and umpire Billy Bowden launched his finger skyward.

The Australians converged on McDonald, embracing him. He'd broken the stubborn seventy-five-minute partnership between Steyn and Makhaya Ntini that had sent the game into the final hour of the Test.

It was a huddle of relief as much as anything else. Australia had started the day needing eight wickets for victory. They'd worn down the defiant visitors one intermittent wicket at a time. Now, finally, despite the resistance of the last pair, it was over.

Except suddenly there was a roar from the SCG crowd. And the beginnings of a standing ovation. This wasn't the cheering of a home crowd celebrating their side's victory, either. It was something else.

Graeme Smith, the South African captain, was coming out to bat with a broken hand.

The Australian backslapping stopped. The huddle dispersed. All celebrations were curtailed. (This was disappointing for Michael Clarke, in particular, who had a party booked. Also for Simon Katich, who had a Clarke-throat-grabbing session booked.) The players made their way back to their fielding positions. The eight final-day wickets they needed to take to win the Test had just become nine.

If the Australians were surprised, they weren't the only ones. Smith himself had arrived at the ground that morning not intending to bat. In addition to the hand that Mitchell Johnson had broken in the first innings, he also had an elbow injury. The elbow was sufficiently damaged that Smith had struggled to brush his teeth that morning.

Furthermore, the dental hygienically challenged Smith had already achieved his goals in this series. For the first time in sixteen years, a side had come to Australia and beaten them in a Test series. The last team to do so had been the West Indies back in 1992/93, who'd achieved the feat thanks to the tightest victory in the history of Tests.

Smith's 2008/09 South African side had not cut it so fine. They'd won the first Test of the series by six wickets, reeling in more than 400 in the final innings in a display of batting dominance. In the second Test, they'd continued that dominance to win by nine wickets. With the series victory secured, there was no need for Smith to risk any further damage to his hand or elbow.

And yet out he marched, wearing a shirt borrowed from Jacques Kallis, with pads strapped on by Morne Morkel. Smith, with an injection in his elbow and fresh plaque on his teeth, was going to bat.

The SCG crowd applauded him all the way to the middle. It's one thing to come to a cricket ground to watch athletes born with extraordinary hand-eye coordination perform feats in which they coordinate those hands and eyes in extraordinary fashion. To witness an attempt at those same feats from a player in severe pain is a rarer sight.

A mummified Rick McCosker famously came out to bat during the Centenary Test in 1977, his broken jaw bandaged to his baggy green. The crowd sang 'Waltzing McCosker' in admiration. The injured opener helped Rod Marsh to a ton and Australia to a match-winning third-innings total.

In 2002, Anil Kumble replicated McCosker's broken-jawed heroics. He returned to the field to bowl against the West Indies in a Test match in Antigua after being struck in the face while batting. His head was bandaged like McCosker's, but he lacked the assistance of a parochial home crowd Weird Al'ing the lyrics to a pseudo-national anthem. Despite this, Kumble sent down fourteen consecutive overs, before flying home the next day for surgery. He remains the only Test bowler to have taken the wicket of Brian Lara while bowling with a broken jaw.

What Kumble achieved with quality of wickets taken while injured Malcolm Marshall did with quantity. In a Test between England and the West Indies in 1984, Marshall broke his left thumb while fielding in the gully. Despite this, when the West Indies batted, he came in at number eleven to partner Larry Gomes as he completed a century. Marshall, batting one-handed, struck a four before he was the last man dismissed. (He then took 7/53 with the ball, because he was Malcolm freaking Marshall, a serious candidate to be the greatest fast bowler in the history of the game.)

Graeme Smith had no intention of batting one-handed. This was because he didn't have a single hand with which to bat. He could hardly bend his right elbow, and he could barely grip with his left hand. But his team had fought their way to within fifty deliveries of a glorious draw. And Smith was not the kind of man who was going to let their efforts come to naught.

And so Smith faced up to the rest of the over from Andrew McDonald, pulling his left hand away from the bat after each defensive stroke.

But if Smith was a hard-nosed leader of a cricket side, determined never to give an inch, so too was Australian captain Ricky Ponting. Ntini survived the next over from Doug Bollinger, thanks to a dropped chance in the slips from Matthew Hayden. So Ponting tossed the ball to Johnson. Smith would get no favours from the Australian skipper.

Smith faced up to the man who had broken his hand. He saw off the over, leaving the balls that were wide of the stumps and jamming down on the yorkers that were on target.

With the final minutes of the match ebbing away, Ponting continued to juggle his bowlers (not literally – he lacked the requisite upper-body strength). He brought both Peter Siddle and Nathan Hauritz back on to bowl and switched the end from which Johnson was bowling so he could target the long crack that was splitting the pitch in two.

It was this last move that did the trick. Bowling over the wicket to the left-handed and broken-handed Smith, the second ball of Johnson's twenty-fourth over hit the crack. It zipped away, beating Smith's bat and crashing into the off stump.

His wicket was shattered. His hopes of saving the Test were in ruins. His hand was still broken. His elbow was as buggered as when he'd begun the day. But Smith's reputation as one of the toughest to ever play the game? That remained fully intact. Yet another example of the variety of ways in which cricket can compel.

From balls of the century to hat-tricks, from classic catches to batting masterclasses, cricket is a team sport that has intermittent feats of individual heroics at its core. Heroics not just of cricketing skill and athleticism but also of mental dominance and courage under fire. And cricket fans never know which kind they'll get. They just know that there's a chance they might witness any one of those feats, at any point. These occasional, unpredictable moments of excellence are what sparks a love of the game in anybody who takes the time to understand it.

NEXT:

How easy is cricket to understand? Exploring the Laws of Cricket. Plus, shrug emoticons!

THE
LAWS
OF
CRICKET

BRIAN JOHNSTON

TALKS ABOUT 'HOLDING WILLEYS'

Terminology

THE MOMENT:

During the fifth Test between England and the West Indies in 1976, commentator Brian Johnston prepares fans for the next delivery by declaring that 'the bowler is Holding, the batsman's Willey'

One of the first ways cricket challenges fledgling fans is by having the Laws of the game use the same terminology to describe as many different elements of the sport as possible. This is the sporting equivalent of having a cackling troll demanding you solve an incomprehensible riddle before you enter.

In 1957, linguist Noam Chomsky theorised that humans are able to learn languages as children because we're genetically encoded with something he called a 'universal grammar'. In essence, we're born with an innate understanding of how language works. It's our environment that determines the specific language in which we first become fluent, be that English, Hindi, Dothraki or emoji.

If this theory is correct, then the language of cricket is best learnt as a child. That's when our minds are most open to deciphering how 'stumps' can be a noun referring to the end of the day's play ('What are you planning to do after *stumps*, Warnie?'), but also a verb referring to the act in which a wicketkeeper dismisses a batter outside of their crease ('Look how Ian Healy so skilfully *stumps* Mark Butcher there, picking up Michael Bevan's leg-side wide on the half-volley in one smooth action'), and finally a different kind of noun that might refer to the pieces of wood stuck in the ground at either end of the pitch ('Oh no! Len Pascoe has picked up one of the *stumps* and is threatening to impale Dilip Doshi with it. This is a little bit disappointing').

That third definition of 'stump' is synonymous with 'wicket'. But 'wicket' is also homonymous with 'wicket', which can also mean the dismissal of a batter (who might have been stumped). But of course a wicket is also – in a piece of terminology designed to be as confusing as possible – the area of the ground *between* the wickets ('Megan Schutt was at great risk of running on the *wicket* because she was bowling *wicket*-to-*wicket*').

You could get around that third definition of wicket by instead calling that area between the wickets or the stumps 'the pitch'. That term has the advantage in that it only has one alternative meaning in cricket. Namely, the point where a delivery bounces ('Didn't that ball *pitch* outside leg stump, Tim? I know we need to get Stokes out, but isn't this a waste of a review?'). A term that has only one variant meaning is one fewer than 'stumps' or 'wicket'. That's good, but it's still one more than any sensibly defined sporting term would ideally possess.

There are many other cricketing terms with multiple meanings, of course. Take 'covers', for example.

That's either a fielding position on the off side or a kind of raincoat for the pitch/wicket. ('Let's get the *covers* onto the field' means something very different to 'Let's get them to field in the *covers*'.)

'Drop'? You can bat at first drop. You can drop a catch. You can be dropped from the side. Sometimes all three in one match.

'Strike rate'? Well, that's either a statistic that measures how devastating a batter is (how many runs they tend to score, on average, in every 100 deliveries), or a statistic that measures how devastating a bowler is (how many balls, on average, it takes for them to get a wicket). Neither version of 'strike rate' should be confused with the batting or bowling average, by the way. Those, at least, have the decency to have the same calculation method (number of runs per wicket). If you want the equivalent of a batting strike rate for a bowler, that's called an 'economy rate'. And it's no longer measured on a 100-ball scale, but on a six-ball scale. Pretty much any glossary of terms for cricket should come with a shrug emoticon included:

¯_(ツ)_/¯

But while all these multiple meanings may seem confusing at first, they also serve to broaden the appeal of cricket. A sport so dominated by numbers could become something of interest only to those with a mathematical bent. However, the flexibility of the terminology opens the door to the kind of wordplay that appeals to those with a bent more inclined to the non-'rithmetic members of the 'three Rs' triad.

It's not just the jargon of the sport that offers such fertile ground for wordplay, either. The players of the sport get into the entendre business as well.

Australia of the mid-1990s was a great cricket side, yes. But it was also a side rife with double-meaning potential. Australia went to Waugh. Opposition sides were Warned. Sometimes there was a May Day alert. It was a newspaper headline writer's dream team.

But the best known application of double meanings of cricketer names came in 1976, when England's middle-order batter Peter Willey faced the express bowling of legendary West Indies speedster Michael Holding.

'The bowler is Holding, the batsman's Willey,' as delivered by Brian Johnston is a near-perfect piece of wordplay. It's clever enough to charm sophisticates, yet childish enough to appeal to lovers of dick jokes. It's not forced – substituting any two names would provide a valid snippet of commentary. The image it evokes is clear and naughty and funny, but the penis euphemism is so mild that nobody could take genuine offence.

Which is why it's a shame that Johnston's legendary piece of commentary never actually happened.

This was confirmed at Johnston's funeral in 1994, after an attempt was made to find the audio of the moment to use as part of his memorial service. Despite trawling through every single delivery that Johnston commentated while Willey faced up to Holding, the renowned phrase was nowhere to be found. The only reference to it came from a prank letter later read on air which complained about the supposed gaffe. One imagines the letter was an after-the-fact realisation of a joke they *should have made*.

Still, it's not too late to rectify this oversight. Admittedly, the 21st-century version is a little more confronting than the original, but we can only work with what we have.

Peter Willey's son David has been a regular Big Bash participant for the past several years. And so too has Ben Cutting.

'The bowler's Cutting, the batter's Willey' is right there for a courageous enough contemporary commentator. Let's see a modern-day Johnston

take a proper stab at it. Enough circumspection.

NEXT:

The language of cricket is fun. But the concepts of cricket are even more so. Plus, Frankie Valli trumpet solos!

SHANE WATSON

REVIEWS HIS FINAL LBW

Leg Before Wicket

THE MOMENT:

In his final Test for Australia, in 2015, Shane Watson is out twice LBW, reviewing on both occasions and having each review dismissed by the third umpire

Explanations of how to play cricket start off simple. One player has a bat, another has a ball. The one with the ball is trying to hit the neatly arranged trio of sticks behind the one with the bat. The one with the bat is trying to prevent this. Easy.

From there, it degenerates almost immediately.

'Okay,' says the newcomer. 'So the one with the ball runs in and throws it at—'

'I'll stop you there,' says the veteran, chuckling in their superior knowledge. 'They don't *throw* it . . .'

And we're away, into the intricacies of bowling with a straight arm. Which leads to no balls and front feet and how you can't be out off a no ball. Unless, of course, you're run out. That then leads to discussions of runs, which leads to leg byes, which then will get you to the almighty hurdle of leg before wicket.

The LBW law is a microcosm of the game itself. It starts off simple. If a bowler is good enough to beat the bat with a delivery and that delivery would have hit the stumps, then the batter should probably still be out, even if their oafish underpinnings got in the way. That's easy enough to comprehend.

But then more complications are added. Talk soon turns to concepts such as 'hitting in line' and 'pitching outside leg'. Then 'was there a little edge on it?' and 'was the batter playing a shot?' – all of which can lead the cricketing novice to a state of bafflement.

And that's before we even begin to contemplate the philosophical implications of an LBW decision. Namely, that the umpire is giving a batter out based not on an event that *did* happen, but an event they believe *would have* happened, if the event that *did* happen (the ball hitting the pads) had *not* happened. A simple aspect of the sport opens the door to a multiverse of parallel realities, like a Large Hadron Collider or a Doctor Strange movie.

These days the umpire's attempts to traverse those alternate timelines is often assisted (or sometimes completely undercut) by ball-tracking. Sophisticated space technology extrapolates the path of the ball to determine where it might have ended up had it not been for that annoying pad.

LBW reviews are commonplace these days. So much so that the most satisfying dismissal in the modern game is surely an LBW that is *not* reviewed when the option to do so is still available.

But such non-reviewed LBWs are rare. Almost always, a batter given out to a ball that has hit the pad is the precursor to a review, should the team have any left. (And a sad, befuddled, extended stare at the umpire if it doesn't.)

All of which brings us to Shane Watson, who wielded an LBW–Review–Decision Upheld–Sad Exit routine like nobody before him.

Watson was an excellent cricketer. No cricketer has ever won as many Australian Player of the Year awards as Watson. A colossus of a man who clubbed the ball with immense power, he was the first Australian to hit centuries in all three forms of the game.

But Watson was not without flaws. He was sluggish between the wickets, prone to injury and determined to showcase his guitar-playing on Instagram. But his biggest flaw was an enormous, immobile front pad. A front pad that drew the ball to it like ridicule to a cricketer playing a guitar on Instagram.

Of batters who've played more than 100 Test innings, nobody was dismissed LBW more often than Watson. Of his 109 innings, he was out LBW on twenty-nine occasions, 26.6 per cent of the time. (Second is Graham Gooch, who fell in this

fashion 23.3 per cent of the time. From 215 Test innings, Gooch was out LBW on exactly fifty occasions – at least thirty of which must have been to Terry Alderman during the 1989 Ashes.)

Watson LBW'ed and reviewed right to the very end of his Test career, with his final Test, in Cardiff, topped by a pair of such dismissals.

Here's the thing, though. As fitting and comical as such a farewell seemed, the fact is that Watson using the reviews in those instances was justified. In the first innings, Australia were 6/265 when he was dismissed, in pursuit of England's 430. Watson had reached 30, early on the third day. It was the seventy-second over in an era when the rule was that DRS reviews were all renewed after the eightieth over. There were two reviews remaining and Watson was the last specialist batter. To not seek to overturn the decision would have been foolish.

The second innings was even more clear-cut. Set 412 to win, Australia had slumped to 6/122 when Brad Haddin was out. Again, Watson was the last remaining batter, trying to see out the fourth day, knowing that rain was forecast for the fifth. So when he was given out before tea, with two reviews remaining, again it made sense for him to try his luck with the ball-tracking. The fact that the decision went against him didn't mean the gamble was not worth taking.

Even the Barmy Army farewelling him by singing 'L-B, L-B, L-B-W' to the tune of the trumpet solo in Frankie Valli's song 'Can't Take My Eyes Off You' didn't change the correctness of the gamble.

Despite jokes to the contrary, Shane Watson understood the LBW law (and let's face it, he'd had plenty of opportunities to study it over his career). He also understood the logic behind reviewing on these two occasions. He probably even knew how likely it was that the reviews would go against him. And how he would therefore be an object of ridicule for many fans, most of whom didn't understand any of these things to the extent that he did. He may have even had an inkling that these might be the final acts he took as a Test cricketer; the Watson Era was coming to a close, allowing for the dawn of the Mitch Marsh Epoch.

Yet he did it anyway. That's the kind of bizarre and counterintuitive heroism that only a deep understanding of the Laws of Cricket gives you.

And that's why it's worth even the most befuddled of newcomers persevering in their attempts to understand the game. Well, that and every other reason I'm about to give in the rest of this section.

NEXT:

Shane Watson regularly fell foul of DRS, yet never gave up on it. Others were not quite so forgiving. Plus, ICC graffiti!

CHETESHWAR PUJARA SUCCESSFULLY USES DRS

DRS

THE MOMENT:

After almost a decade of resistance, India agree to use DRS in a 2016 Test series against England, enabling Cheteshwar Pujara to overturn an LBW decision and go on to make a century

India were one of the first teams to volunteer to be part of the Umpire Decision Review System. (The Umpire Decision Review System is abbreviated to DRS, rather than UDRS. The lack of the U stresses the system's central role in removing umpires from the game.)

In 2008, in a series against Sri Lanka, India trialled the DRS. Over the course of that series, they were successful with just one review out of twenty attempts. India might have reacted to this outcome by trying to get better at using the technology or working to improve the system (there *were* teething problems). Instead, their superstar players graffitied 'DRS sux' on the walls of ICC headquarters and refused to ever use it again. A bold and unruly stand.

This led to almost a full decade of inconsistency in international cricket, with every other nation DRS'ing their brains out while India stubbornly abstained.

Over time, however, Anil Kumble, Sachin Tendulkar, MS Dhoni and friends grew old. And Virat Kohli, a god-in-ascendance, unscarred by that original Sri Lanka series, rose in power. With Kohli's holy blessing, DRS was employed in the India–England series in 2016.

(The unification of DRS left only one reigning source of international cricketing inconsistency. That was Australia saying the score the opposite way to everybody else: '3 for 50' rather than '50 for 3'. Testify, my baggy green comrades!)

It took three days for the DRS-approving India side to reap its rewards. The man who did so was Cheteshwar Pujara, who overturned an LBW when given out on 86. He went on to score 124. It didn't change the result, which was a high-scoring draw. But it proved that DRS wasn't fundamentally anti-India.

But those eight years spent trying to convince India that DRS was legit can never be regained. In an alternative timeline, DRS might be so well established by now that we could have moved into meta-gaming strategies. Perhaps DRS reviews could have evolved into a form of currency. Imagine a cricketing world where you could trade a review to win the toss. Or save up five reviews over the course of a series to get the automatic wicket of the opposition's best batter.

No doubt all that will come, and cricket will be better for it. For now, however, we're still stuck with the basics of DRS. A world with everybody squabbling about the fundamentals. Where naysayers still get worked up about things they perceive as broken.

Which is a shame. Because DRS isn't broken. In fact, it's pretty close to as good as it can reasonably get. Yet people continue to propose changes to it.

One of the common suggestions is that DRS should be taken out of players' hands and implemented by the umpires. This is a flawed concept (at least, for now). The time taken to review a decision is too long to apply to every appeal. If the umpires sent every appeal upstairs, the actual amount of cricket played would shrink away to nothing. And of course, if you've seen how umpires deal with run-outs, you know that if given control of the DRS, they *would* send every appeal to the third umpire.

Rightly so, too. Because the first time the umpires didn't review a decision and were later shown to be wrong, the team on the wrong end of that decision would lose their collective minds. And if that team were India, we could lose another decade to them re-boycotting it.

No, the true value of DRS is how it transfers attention away from umpires' mistakes and onto players' mistakes. A bad umpiring decision becomes a bad team decision for having no reviews remaining. This kind of blame-shifting is a form of alchemy. One that places cricket at the cutting edge of television decision-making assistance. (Plus, it lets us properly revel in teams' misfortune when they receive a howler immediately after burning their reviews. Sweet, delicious schadenfreude.)

The other thing many fans and commentators feel needs changing in DRS comes from the exact opposite perspective. Instead of wanting more power for the umpires, they want less. More specifically, they want to remove the 'umpire's call' from the process. 'How can the same delivery be in or out depending on the umpire's opinion?' these folk exclaim in exasperation, cheerily overlooking every single umpiring decision in the history of cricket before the introduction of DRS.

'Either the ball's hitting the stumps or not,' they'll often add, again in full defiance of the fact that any projection has an inherent uncertainty built into it. All that can be offered are probabilities, not certainties. Even the plumbest of LBWs could be undone by a wayward kamikaze seagull. Heck, in a quantum universe it's even possible, in principle, for the ball to *transform into* a kamikaze seagull. (That is so utterly, stupidly unlikely that the boffins generally don't include it in the modelling, but it's there.)

Granted, these are unlikely events, but even smaller factors – such as a gust of wind or slight measurement errors in determining the exact position of the ball along its trajectory – can introduce errors to the projections. And no matter how small the errors, there is no avoiding the possibility of a fifty-fifty case. Say the ball tracking measures the ball's future path to within 1 millimetre accuracy, for example. In that case, all you need is for that path to be projected to pass the stumps by, say, half a millimetre. Suddenly, your super-accurate ball tracking is not much help in determining whether the ball will clip the stumps or not.

With this understanding, it's perhaps clearer that any graphic that shows 'half a ball' hitting the stump is misleading. 'Half a ball hitting' is better understood as a *50 per cent likelihood* that the ball is hitting the stump. Maybe it's missing. Maybe it's hitting. But if the ball tracking is teetering between two equally (or even equally-ish) likely possibilities, then the most sensible way of breaking that tie is by going with the umpire. Yes, if it's *that* tight they may be guessing too. But they're the closest person to the scene who doesn't have a vested interest in the outcome. Give them something to do.

Now, the more accurate the ball tracking gets, the less likely it is that these 'too close to call' projections will arise. Are we at that point yet? Maybe. But if we are, then everybody must also agree to give up on the eyebrows-raised disbelief when that same ball-tracking software suggests the ball was bouncing more than everybody thought. It can't be both super-accurate *and* occasionally wacky. Choose your lane.

At the time of writing, the forces opposed to umpire's call seem to be rising in prominence. Will they have removed it from DRS by the time this book is published, rendering these last few hundred words moot? Or will the pro–umpire's call adherents have argued those forces back into befuddled submission?

Impossible to say. Let's go with the editor's call.

NEXT:

The first area of cricket to get television assistance was run-outs. Not that Jonty Rhodes needed television assistance to make a run-out thrilling. Plus, lumbering pickles!

JONTY RHODES

CRASHES THROUGH THE STUMPS

Run-outs

THE MOMENT:
South Africa celebrates their last-minute
inclusion in the 1992 World Cup by having
Jonty Rhodes crash *through* the stumps to
run out Pakistan batter Inzamam-ul-Haq

There are two types of run-outs. The first is the run-out where both batters are in agreement that they should be going for the run, only to be undone by a piece of fielding brilliance.

For example, Pat Cummins ending a full day in the field by swooping on a ball and dive-flinging it into the side of the stumps to run out the previously mentioned Cheteshwar Pujara on 123. That's an arresting display of athleticism. But it's not as if we didn't already know that Cummins was a superhuman creature rocketed to our planet as an infant. Elite athletes performing elite feats of athleticism is par for the elite course in professional (aka elite) sport. Go back to the first section of the book if you want to read about those kinds of antics.

But the other type of run-out showcases some of the more nuanced aspects of cricket. This is the run-out where the skill of the fielder plays little or no part in the dismissal.

There are two types of these unskilled-fielder run-outs.

The first are the run-outs where the batters are in agreement with one another on the viability of a run. In these run-outs, circumstances conspire in such a way to still bring one of them undone.

Usually, such batter-agreed, unskilled-fielder run-outs arise from unluckiness and/or confusion which leaves a batter stranded. In the good old days, this kind of confusion was often caused by the presence of a runner for an injured batter. (Runners were a supposed benefit that were secretly a hindrance. Like, for example, a cursed scimitar in *Dungeons and Dragons*, or Zack Snyder agreeing to take charge of your superhero cinematic universe.)

Runners are much missed. But even without them, the modern game still has potential for run-out confusion. Sometimes, for example, batters collide while running between wickets. More often, a batter will be run out after backing up too far. A straight drive will deflect off the bowler's fingertips – or the face of Adam Zampa – and into the stumps. All the non-striker can do is despair at what is invariably described by commentators as the unluckiest way for a batter to be dismissed. Y'know, as if we'd all somehow forgotten that Xavier Doherty took 72 international wickets.

Sometimes the batter isn't unlucky or confused, but careless and inattentive. Which could lead to a mankad – which technically is a form of run-out. And one into which we don't have the time to delve any deeper here. (There will, however, be more on mankads in the next section. Promise.)

These unskilled-fielder run-outs where the batters are in agreement are compelling. But they don't compare to the thrills offered in the versions where the batters disagree.

What makes batter-opposed, unskilled-fielder run-outs such a thrilling part of the game is that we get to see real-time negotiations from players who are ostensibly working in partnership for the same team. It's a display of social dynamics that gives us a glimpse into the personalities and standing of the players involved. A batter saying 'no' to a partner already halfway down the pitch is expressing dominance as surely as a silverback gorilla beating his chest or a person misspelling their spouse's name on the divorce papers.

It takes a certain amount of ego to succeed as a professional sportsperson. So it's hardly surprising that these negotiations can rapidly escalate to reach fraught and exhilarating heights. In most cases, one of the pair backs down and accedes to the other's decision on whether a run should be attempted or not.

Adding spice to the situation, the quicker the non-dominant batting partner acquiesces to their stronger-willed colleague, the more likely that submissive batter is to survive the moment of disagreement. (Although they're still not as likely to survive as if they stick to their original decision and force their teammate to be the one who backs down.)

This all makes for a beautiful system that devolves into a game of chicken. And this takes place between two cricketers, who, lest we forget, are theoretically on the same side.

In an ideal case, both will be stubborn enough that neither will change their mind. In this case, we end up with the apex of run-out disagreements: both batters running for the same end. The most exquisite display of team sport individualism one could hope for.

And there is potential for this kind of ego-driven shambles every. single. ball. Magnificent. The sole improvement one could make to these kind of run-outs would be for the scorers to attribute the wicket to one of the batters. Just to raise the stakes a little higher.

The undisputed king of these kind of run-outs (and pretty much every other kind too) was Pakistan's inept running genius Inzamam-ul-Haq. Sure, others may have been run out 'more often' than Inzamam. But that's just numbers. And numbers are for the weak of heart. Inzamam was run out *better* than anybody else in the history of the game.

His most notorious run-out was the second one that befell him. Five days after his twenty-second birthday, playing his twelfth ODI in his first World Cup, Inzamam was struck on the pad, trying to lift the ball to the leg side. Pakistan were 2/135, chasing a rain-reduced target of 194 from 36 overs. And Inzamam was batting quickly, having reached 48 from 44 balls.

What Inzamam *wasn't* doing quickly, however, was moving between the wickets. After the ball struck his pad, he lumbered a couple of querulous paces down the pitch. Perhaps there was a leg bye on offer? Non-striker Imran Khan disagreed, sending him back. And since Imran was the captain, the disagreement was resolved in his favour.

Which put the slow-turning Inzamam in a lumbering pickle. Because South African fielder Jonty Rhodes had swooped onto the ball from backward point.

Completing the run-out didn't need fielding brilliance. At least, not in traditional terms, where one theatrically intercepts the ball and throws down the stumps from an acute angle.

No, the only brilliance required from Rhodes was the realisation that he was much, much (much) faster than Inzamam. Once that sank in, his best course of action was clear. And spectacular. He sprinted towards the stumps, homing in on them with every speedy step.

Inzamam, meanwhile, had almost completed his turn. In a few minutes he would begin retracing the pair of steps required to regain his crease.

But it was all far too late. Rhodes had already closed most of the gap between himself and the stumps. He breached the final part of it with a full-length leap that saw him crash *through* the stumps, scattering them everywhere.

If the stumps symbolically represent the batter's wicket (in the sense of them being in), then Inzamam was more out than anybody had ever been.

(Inzamam would redeem himself with a player-of-the-match innings of 60 from 37 balls – run out, of course – in the semi-final, to send Pakistan through to a final they'd win. Rhodes's semi-final experience was less happy, as the rain rules forsook South Africa.)

South Africa had been a last-minute addition to the World Cup, their international exile ending along with apartheid. Five matches into their tournament, this stumps-splaying run-out was as dramatic an announcement of their return to world cricket as was possible to make. It ushered in a new era of international cricket.

Jonty Rhodes had arrived, a fielder ready and willing to create run-outs out of nothing. Inzamam-ul-Haq had arrived, a batter ready and willing to do the same. Cricket would be greater for the presence of both.

NEXT:

Seven years later, another great South African fielder in a World Cup. But this time, one who couldn't keep the ball in his hand. Plus, Zoom call bathroom breaks!

HERSCHELLE GIBBS

DROPS THE WORLD CUP

Ball Control

THE MOMENT:

Chasing 272 for victory in order to make
the semi-finals of the 1999 World Cup,
Australian captain Steve Waugh hits the
ball to Herschelle Gibbs, who drops the
ball as he goes to celebrate

In July 1999, after a shaky start, Australia's World Cup campaign had – to quote the monotone words of Lisa Simpson dorothy-dixing gubernatorial candidate Monty Burns – developed the momentum of a runaway freight train.

Like any decent runaway train, there was the sense that the entire thing could career off the rails at any moment. This was precisely why it was such a stirring campaign to follow for bleary-eyed fans back home.

Shane Warne shared that sense of imminent derailment. But he also had a solution. The night before Australia played South Africa at Headingley in the last Super Six game, Warne told his teammates to stand their ground if Herschelle Gibbs took a catch.

His rationale was twofold. Firstly, Gibbs had taken to discarding the ball in faux-cool fashion after taking a catch. The act was designed to demean the caught batter. *Your wicket is not even worth celebrating* – this was the message behind Gibbs's contemptuous casting aside of the ball. So quick was Gibbs's disdainful dispensing that if the slightest thing went wrong with his posturing, the catch could be transformed into a drop under the laws of the game.

Secondly, because Warne was an actual living wizard, he had foreseen that Gibbs would do *exactly that* the very next day.

And so Herschelle Gibbs dropped the World Cup.

(Much like Brian Johnston's 'Holding Willey' comment, the claim that Steve Waugh told Gibbs that he'd 'dropped the World Cup' does not stand up to scrutiny. The actual response from Waugh to Gibbs's drop was something more like 'I hope you realise that you've just lost the game for your team'. However, the upgraded line is so much better than this original that it's the one rightly enshrined in the cricket narrative. Accurate historical transcriptions are for other, lesser sports. Cricket, a sport that attracts wordsmiths, deserves a rewrite option.)

The Gibbs drop also served as another example of the nit-picking precision of the Laws of Cricket. Much like every other area of the game, the concept of a catch starts off simple. If a batter hits the ball in the air and a fielder catches it, then they're out. But things get more and more complicated as the laws try to clarify all the edge cases.

Where can your feet be in relationship to the boundary when you're taking a catch? What happens if the catch ricochets off another fielder? Or the other batter? Or an umpire? Or a bird? Can you catch it between your legs? How about in your pocket? In your cap?

And, most relevantly for the Gibbs effort: how long do you need to hold the catch for it to count? Because Gibbs held the flick off Waugh's pads for a *long* time. According to the stopwatch, it was only about a third of a second, but that's a long time for a catch. (And it seemed much longer on the slow-motion replay, as is so often the case.)

It turns out there's no minimum time a catch needs to be held. Instead, the laws advise that the player must have complete control over the ball, something that Gibbs did not. Although it's possible that, had Gibbs held his cool, he might have got away with it. Instead, he adopted the facial reaction of a Zoom meeting attendee who's just realised they didn't mute their trip to the bathroom.

It's remarkable to think that the validity of a catch that changed the course of a World Cup hinged on whether a fielder broke character or not.

It should come as no surprise that the Laws of Cricket *also* have a section related to the kind of fielder bluffing that, in retrospect, Gibbs should have employed. The fake fielding law was introduced to stop fielders from pretending they had the ball or were closer to the ball than they actually were, thereby bluffing batters out of taking runs. It doesn't *really* apply to fielders pretending they had greater control of the disposal of the ball than they actually did.

But even if it did, it wouldn't have affected this 1999 match. The fake fielding law was only introduced in 2017. The first fielder to receive a penalty for it was playing for Queensland in a domestic limited-overs match against CAXI. CAXI was a Cricket Australia eleven of promising young players sent out to be thrashed by more experienced state sides. To build character or something. And the wily old Queensland fielder penalised for attempting to trick those gullible young batters by faking a throw at the stumps when he didn't have the ball? That would be 23-year-old Marnus Labuschagne.

Yes, *that* Marnus Labuschagne. (You didn't really think there were two of them, did you?)

It seems fitting that Labuschagne was the first cricketer penalised for fake fielding. He later became the first cricketer to be a concussion substitute when he replaced Steve Smith in the 2019 Ashes.

Labuschagne is a cricketer who, in the grand clichéd tradition, 'makes things happen'. And even when he's taking some well-earned time away from the things-happening manufacturing business, things still seem to happen *around* him.

He began his Test career against Pakistan in 2018, with one catch already in the bank thanks to a grab as a substitute fielder back in 2014. Always inspiring when a cricketer has stats on the board before their Test debut. Indeed, at one stage he had the following magnificently silly stats:

Tests: 1

Wickets: 1

Catches: 1

Substitute catches: 1

Warnings for running on the pitch: 1

Runs: 0

This from a man selected to bat at number six. It's as if a computer was programmed to come up with a cricketer and had only one bit to specify each of the key data points.

Labuschagne has gone on to greater things since that bit part start. And Gibbs went on to greater things too after his ill-famed drop. Most notably, he anchored the greatest one-day run chase of all time, scoring 175 from 111 balls when South Africa ran down Australia's 434.

But their key moments – at least for the purposes of this section of the book – demonstrate how, between the two of them, they establish the vast breadth of coverage of the Laws of Cricket.

Maybe you don't have control of the release of a ball. Maybe you have control of the release of a ball you don't have. Either way, the Laws of Cricket are going to get you.

NEXT:

The wide-ranging Laws of Cricket need umpires to enforce them. What happens when the umpires' senses betray them? Plus, hanged munchkins!

DARRELL HAIR
NO-BALLS
MUTTIAH
MURALITHARAN

Chucking

THE MOMENT:

On the first day of the 1995 Boxing Day
Test between Australia and Sri Lanka,
umpire Darrell Hair no-balls Muttiah
Muralitharan for chucking

Let's get one thing straight: there's nothing inherently crooked about chucking.

That's not actually true, of course. The act of chucking, by its very definition, contains an arm that is crooked. But the crookedness of a chucked delivery exists only in that very limited literal definition. There is no implication of crookedness in the broader sense of an illegality being committed.

Although that's not, in fact, true either. A chucked delivery *is* an illegal delivery. That's why the umpires were encouraged, for most of the history of cricket, to no-ball a bowler who they spotted wielding a bent arm. Much like they'd no-ball one whose foot went too far over the popping crease. 'Sorry about that, champion. Let me pop an extra onto the scorecard and you can have another crack.'

Except that's not true either, is it? Because when a bowler oversteps and is called for a no ball, there might be a miffed shake of the head or the occasional pantomime re-enactment of the incident as the umpire demonstrates to the befuddled bowler how far they were over the line. However, there will rarely be any further repercussions for the front-foot no-balling.

Whereas if you were no-balled for chucking, you know what tended to break loose? That's right, hell. And do you know how much of hell broke loose? That's right, *all* of it.

That's what happened in 1995 when Darrell Hair called Muttiah Muralitharan.

The rule not to bend one's arm while bowling has existed for as long as overarm bowling has existed. (To be more precise, you can bowl with a bent arm as long as you don't straighten it in the delivery action.)

The straight arm restriction served as a limiter on how fast bowlers could deliver the ball. The cricketing lawmakers in 1864 who had been persuaded to permit overarm bowling presumably still wanted some method of preventing bowlers from sprinting in and throwing the ball at a batter with all their might.

One imagines that other options for limiting the speed of overarm bowling were considered and rejected. Perhaps run-ups could have been outlawed, forcing the bowler to stand still and throw it at the other end. This would have been an excellent way to pre-empt baseball, which was due to be invented in 1869. A no-run-up policy, had it been adopted, would have also been helpful in modern times in the combating of slow over rates.

Or maybe overarm throwing could have been permitted if bowlers had to throw it with their non-dominant hand. Such a rule would be difficult to police, of course. But getting bowlers to sign affidavits on which hand was their dominant one would have done the trick. Especially if it was noted in what hand they held the pen while doing so. Although, this would still have been open to ambidextrous exploitation (aka ambidexploitation).

Instead of these or other options, the preferred method for putting a handbrake on overarm bowling was the enforcement of the straight arm.

This went more or less smoothly for the next 125 years. Oh, sure, the occasional bowler was called for chucking. For example, Ian Meckiff, who was no-balled four times for chucking in a Test against South Africa in 1963. Meckiff reacted to this by retiring from all cricket immediately after the match concluded.

Meckiff's rapid adieu was reportedly due to the rabid ado that surrounded chucking. To chuck was to commit a grievous sin against cricket. Even the word 'chucking' itself evoked something nauseating.

Worse still, 'chucking' transcended verb status. Because a bowler did not merely chuck the ball. That would imply it was an act that could be curtailed, like overstepping the crease. No, a transgressing bowler was 'a chucker' – an all-encompassing noun that defined them. A chucker had no place on a cricket field, in much the same way that a notional 'overstepper' would be rendered pointless.

Yet despite the precedent set by Meckiff, the Sri Lanka side of 1995, led by the combative Arjuna Ranatunga, had no intention of abandoning their young spinner. Understandably, given he was their most powerful attacking weapon.

And this is where chucking becomes one of the things that make cricket so great.

The triple-jointed Murali was sent for testing by biomechanics experts. They discovered that his arm did bend (or 'flex') as he delivered the ball. But – and here's the rub – so did every other bowler's.

Chucking was no longer a binary thing. Bowlers didn't chuck or not. They *all* bent their arm to some degree. The decision now was where to put that degree cut-off.

The powers-that-be settled on fifteen. Fifteen degrees of bend was allowed. And the tests showed that Murali was within that margin.

Indeed, in one powerful televised demonstration in 2004, Murali bowled with his arm in a rigid steel brace. The brace prevented him from transgressing the fifteen-degree barrier. But not from bowling his entire repertoire of deliveries. That more or less ended any further discussion for fair-minded people. (Unfair-minded people, of course, continued to hilariously call out 'no ball' from the crowd whenever he bowled for the rest of his career.)

Any appearance that Murali was chucking was an optical illusion. He was the 'vase or two faces' of spin bowling. The 'rabbit or duck'. The 'hanging munchkin in *The Wizard of Oz*.

Whatever your eyes told you was wrong, Murali didn't chuck.

This raised a new issue. Cricket was now telling its officials that they couldn't trust their own senses while they were umpiring. As the 18th-century philosopher Immanuel Kant posited in *The Critique of Pure Reason*, and as Obi-Wan Kenobi clarified further in *Star Wars*, 'your eyes can deceive you, don't trust them'.

Given this ocular deception, umpires would no longer no-ball for chucking on the field. The blast shield for no-ball calls was officially down. Instead, the policy going forward would be to defer any decision. Leave it to specialist biomechanists to determine if bowlers bent their arm beyond the fifteen-degree limit.

Of course, the policy of deferred calling of no balls for chucking means that now any bowler can chuck the ball whenever they want. In a desperate enough last ball situation they could do so, confident that as long as they weren't *too* obvious about it, they wouldn't be called.

In the modern professional era, death bowlers everywhere are no doubt working on this. Practising the twenty-five-degree flex delivery for that exact situation. Something to add to their repertoire of slow bouncers and wide yorkers. Use the extra speed or turn that a chucked delivery will give you to win the match, don't get called for it, apologise later. You know it makes sense.

Murali went on to take 800 Test wickets, more than any other bowler in the history of the game. What's glorious about that is that he didn't just end on a round number. He ended on one of the *roundest* numbers. One gets the impression that he deliberately ended on a number so completely lacking in angles just to make a point.

Much like the rest of his bowling, it was a case of 'weird flex, but okay'.

NEXT:

When the Laws of Cricket are broken, what punishments are invoked? And by whom? Plus, Windows 10 updates!

CAMERON BANCROFT PUTS SANDPAPER DOWN HIS PANTS

Penalties

THE MOMENT:

During the third Test between South Africa and Australia in 2018, Cameron Bancroft is caught by television cameras trying to rough up the ball with sandpaper

Perhaps you remember this scandalous South African moment. A suspicious home television broadcaster was keeping a close eye on the visiting side. They spotted a fielder trying to use something in his pocket to change the condition of the ball, to assist his bowlers to gain reverse swing. The third umpire became aware of the footage and alerted his on-field colleagues. They intervened and investigated further, summoning the fielding captain over for further questioning. Clear evidence of ball tampering was uncovered. Which led to the visitors receiving the ultimate punishment: five (5) penalty runs awarded to the batting side.

I refer, of course, to the disreputable incident in 2013, when South Africa's Faf du Plessis was caught rubbing the ball on the zip of his trousers during a Test against Pakistan.

The five penalty runs awarded to the Pakistan side didn't help them much. They still lost by an innings and 92 runs. But at least it wasn't an innings and 97 runs. That would have been embarrassing.

Penalty runs are the next level up from no balls and wides. (If one wants to be pedantic, no balls and wides are also a form of penalty runs, but they're lower-case penalty runs, not the more serious upper-case Penalty Runs.)

The umpires have the power to wield penalty runs as a punishment for a wide variety of indiscretions. Ball tampering, of course. And fake fielding. But also for such diverse and heinous breaches of the laws as time wasting, returning to the field without permission, damaging the pitch, deliberate short runs, having helmets or other items of clothing hit by the ball, and excessive appealing.

That last item could have been the most interesting avenue to explore back when DRS was first introduced. As discussed, the current system of teams having a set number of reviews to use and then having no recourse to further examination after that is good. But it's not difficult to instead imagine a mechanism with no limits but where a failed review costs a team a certain number of penalty runs. This would have resulted in a cricketing world where teams were less inclined to make frivolous reviews. And would still always allow access to them in the case of a genuine umpiring howler. Alas, that wasn't the way the ICC went. Instead, penalty runs remain a rarely used tool for punishing rarely committed breaches.

Probably a good thing. Because much like Hammurabi or Judge Dredd, when it comes to penalty runs, the on-field umpires are the law.

Teams have no opportunity to appeal the decision.

Pakistan discovered this in 2006 while touring England. That's when umpires Darrell Hair and Billy Doctrove imposed a five-run penalty for ball tampering. The Pakistan side, unhappy with the decision, refused to return to the field after tea. As a result, they were ruled to have forfeited the Test, the only such defeat in Test match history.

So if refusing to play doesn't serve as a practical means of appeal against penalty runs, what does?

One key is the way in which penalty runs are applied. The implication of penalty runs is that they will be subtracted from the infringing team's tally. In fact, this doesn't happen, which is a shame for anybody hopeful of someday seeing a team bowled out for a negative amount of runs. Instead, penalty runs are added to the victimised side's score. If the fielding side receives the penalty runs due to a batting side's indiscretion, then the runs are added to the previous innings. Or if the fielding side hasn't yet batted, to their next innings.

This opens one very specific door for appeal. A batting team that receives penalty runs against them in the first innings of the match could, in principle, bat for five days. If they were able to do so without declaring, their opponents would have no opportunity to accrue said penalty runs. Such an action might seem unsportsmanlike. And that might tempt the umpires to inflict further penalty runs on the batting team. But that just further incentivises the team to double down on their protest.

No, for penalty runs to make sense under all scenarios, they should not apply to any specific innings. Instead, they should live in their own limbo dimension, outside of conventional time and space, like God or a Windows 10 update.

The umpires in the sandpaper incident took none of these penalty run musings into consideration. We know this because the sandpaper hidden in Cameron Bancroft's pants at the encouragement of David Warner and, at best, wilful ignorance of captain Steve Smith earned South Africa precisely zero (0) penalty runs for Australia's tampering. Heck, the umpires didn't even change the ball. The extent of the eventual ICC punishment was a one-match ban for Steve Smith and the loss of his match fee. Bancroft was fined 75 per cent of his match fee. David Warner? No problem, from the ICC's perspective.

So why did the entire incident explode to the extent it did? With

Cricket Australia banning both Smith and Warner from international cricket for a year and Bancroft for nine months?

Two reasons. Firstly, the Australian players' clear intention was to tamper with the ball. This was different to the du Plessis incident in one critical respect. A zipper is part of a pocket – so it was conceivable that the South African could have been rubbing the ball on it without realising. This depends on a willingness to give him the benefit of the doubt. (A willingness that might change if you were able to foresee that, two years later, he'd be busted for applying saliva to the ball with a mint in his mouth.) But if you did give him that benefit, you could chalk the entire incident up to a simple mistake. One worthy of punishment, but with no need to take the incident any further. That was match referee David Boon's position. 'I am also satisfied that this was not part of a deliberate and/or prolonged attempt to unfairly manipulate the condition of the ball,' the non-prescient Boon said. 'And that the imposition of a fine of 50 per cent of his match fee is appropriate considering the circumstances.'

There was no such defence for the Australian actions five years later. Unless you're a contestant on *The Block* – which, based on my detailed

research, Cameron Bancroft has not once ever been – sandpaper is not the kind of thing that you happen to find in your pocket.

Secondly, the Australians were deemed to not merely have violated the Laws of Cricket. They contravened a force far more powerful.

The Laws of Cricket are comprehensive. They take the basics of the sport and examine the logical limitations of them from a myriad of angles. Any fan willing to delve deeper into the sport is therefore rewarded with nuances of the laws all the way down. What is a wicket? What is a catch? What is an LBW? What is a run-out? What is truth?

But the laws still don't fully define the limits of what is acceptable in the sport. Nor the punishments that can be laid down if those acceptable limits are breached. That requires an extra set of regulatory principles.

This second set of guidelines bolsters, extends and sometimes outright contradicts the laws of the game. It is known as the Spirit of Cricket.

NEXT:

We join a Ghostbusting dojo to take on the all-powerful force that haunts the entire sport, the Spirit of Cricket. Plus, the wielding of semicolons!

THE SPIRIT OF CRICKET

ADAM GILCHRIST

WALKS IN A WORLD CUP SEMI-FINAL

Walking

THE MOMENT:

In the Australia v Sri Lanka semi-final of the 2003 World Cup, Adam Gilchrist chooses to walk despite being given not out by umpire Rudi Koertzen for a catch behind the wicket

In cricket, 'walking' refers to a batter who knows they should be given out by the umpire not waiting for that decision. Instead, they walk off, effectively giving themselves out.

It's a trivial idea. But it's one that builds to a genuine philosophical debate that traverses concepts as diverse as probability theory, the nature of truth, and the moral rights of the individual within a group.

The argument for walking is simple. It's an appeal to a player's better instincts, their sense of fair play. If the batter knows they're out, then they should put up their hand, even if the umpire hasn't raised theirs. Umpiring is difficult. It's a good thing for the batter to help them out when they have more information than the umpires do.

The argument against walking requires more unpacking, but starts from similar premises. Yes, umpiring is difficult. Yes, sometimes the batter has more information than the umpires. But walking only resolves one half of the error-making. The half that would have otherwise helped them. The flip side doesn't work. If a batter has more information than the umpire and knows they *didn't* hit it, when the umpire claims they did, then they can't choose to stick around.

It's this bias that the non-walker is looking to counter. Sometimes the umpire errors will be in the batter's favour, sometimes they won't. On average, hopefully, they'll even out. But if the batter negates all the errors in their favour by walking, then the errors *can't* even out. The batter will be given out, overall, more often than they should be.

To be fair, there's an ounce of truth in this logic. Even if that logic counsels against being fair and telling the truth.

In the modern era, of course, none of this should apply anymore. If a player is a top-six batter, they should always have enough reviews left to negate any bad decisions that go against them. If they don't, then they don't have a problem with the umpires. They have a problem with their T-happy teammates batting above them.

With errors against the batter negated by DRS, the sole argument for not walking is removed. Especially since, if a player doesn't walk, they're almost certainly going to be sent off via the opposition's use of DRS anyway.

No, in the modern era of international cricket, it's better to walk and not waste everybody's time.

But in the pre-DRS era, the argument for being a non-walker was solid. What's more, the argument gained greater and greater strength, the longer an international cricketer played. The more innings one had, the more likely it was that the errors from the umpires would, in ordinary circumstances, even out. But not for walkers, who were specifically only leaving themselves with the errors that went against them.

Countering this, if a cricketer had such a lengthy international career, that tended to suggest that they were either (a) pretty handy with the bat, or (b) in the side for reasons other than their batting, or (c) both.

Which brings us neatly to Adam Gilchrist, a man who, in 2003, was as secure in his place in the Australian side as anybody could expect to be. So he decided he could afford to obey his conscience and walk. Even if this sometimes meant he cost himself some sneaky bonus runs because of umpire errors. A fine moral stand.

But – and again, here's the non-walking counter-argument – Gilchrist's runs weren't only being tallied for him. They were also being tallied for Australia. Maybe it's fine for Gilchrist to decide that he'd rather cost himself some runs than compromise his principles. But did he have a

right to cost his team runs in order to assuage his own sense of guilt?

Which brings us, only marginally less neatly, to Gilchrist's captain at the time, Ricky Ponting.

To set the scene, Australia had tediously not lost a match throughout the entire 2003 World Cup tournament. They'd therefore made their way to a semi-final against Sri Lanka.

Australia batted first, and after five overs, openers Gilchrist and Matthew Hayden had put on 34 runs. Aravinda de Silva was introduced to the attack early, and Gilchrist attempted to sweep his second ball. Amid a flurry of bat and front pad, the ball ballooned to keeper Kumar Sangakkara.

Despite raucous appeals from Sri Lanka, umpire Rudi Koertzen shook his head. But Gilchrist knew he'd edged the ball and, to the surprise of everybody, walked. He was replaced by Ponting, who was dismissed next over for two. When Hayden also fell, Australia were 3/51 in the thirteenth over, and in genuine trouble.

Back in the dressing room, Gilchrist and Ponting debated the merits of the former's decision to walk, before putting that aside to help Australia defeat Sri Lanka by 48 runs.

Despite not being in the dressing room to witness the Gilchrist–Ponting walking argument, we can still get a hint of their debate. We do so by consulting their respective massive autobiographies, *True Colours* and *At the Close of Play*.

Ponting spends only half a page on Gilchrist's walking. He calls it 'a peculiar incident in that none of us knew at the time that Gilly had suddenly decided to take the umpiring into his own hands'. Ponting clarified his own views on walking: 'the umpires are there to make the decisions; my role as a batsman was to try to accept the good with the bad'. (As an aside, that's magnificent semicolon usage from Australia's most prolific wielder of the bat.)

Gilchrist, on the other hand, has an entire index entry devoted to walking. The index refers the reader to sixteen different pages on the topic. This includes a lengthy explanation of the World Cup walk, and the cold shoulder he felt he got from his teammates at the time for the decision.

The sixteen different pages mentioned in the index accumulate to approximately ten pages of content. Which means that Gilchrist spends 1.6 per cent of his 627-page autobiography on walking. A hardcover version of Adam Gilchrist's autobiography weighs 1.118 kilograms. Which means that Gilchrist's pro-walking

argument has 17.83 grams of weight attached to it.

In contrast, half a page out of 697 pages is a mere 0.07 per cent of Ricky Ponting's autobiography. Despite Ponting's tome being almost forty grams heavier than Gilchrist's, tipping the kitchen scales at 1.155 kilograms, his anti-walking argument comes in at a mere 0.83 of a gram.

There we are. We have, quite literally, weighed up the pro and anti-walking arguments from Gilchrist and Ponting. Pro-walking wins by seventeen grams. There may not be an ounce of truth that walking is the right thing to do, but there's 0.6 of an ounce. That's close enough, surely.

NEXT:

Ricky Ponting falls afoul of another grey area of sportsmanship. This time, the use of substitute fielders. Plus, kick me signs!

GARY PRATT
RUNS OUT
RICKY PONTING

Substitute Fielders

THE MOMENT:

As Australia tries to save the fourth Test of the 2005 Ashes, after following on for the first time in 191 Tests, England substitute fielder Gary Pratt runs out Ricky Ponting

Australia were regularly in trouble during the 2005 Ashes. Sometimes this was because of injuries to key bowlers. Sometimes because of sudden loss of form of batters. Mostly, though, it was because England rather unsportingly showed up with a team willing to play competitive cricket. A kind of gamesmanship they hadn't tried for a couple of decades.

The most trouble Australia were in was during the fourth Test at Trent Bridge. The series was locked at 1–1 going into the match. However, England had been the better side in the drawn third Test, salvaged only by Ponting's fourth-innings, final-day batting heroics.

Now, in the fourth Test, Glenn McGrath was injured. He'd also been absent in the second Test, after stepping on a cricket ball during pre-game warm-ups. Australia had lost that Test. This fresh lack of McGrath for the fourth Test therefore felt ominous.

So it proved, with England winning the toss, batting first and putting on 477. In the absence of McGrath's control, opening bowlers Brett Lee and Michael Kasprowicz both struggled. They finished with figures of 1/131 and 1/122. (Lee got the former, Kasprowicz the latter. Not that it made much difference.)

More ominous was Australia's batting in reply. The top order

collapsed to 3/22, and could only recover to 218 all out, 60 runs short of the follow-on target. England captain Michael Vaughan enforced the follow-on. One imagines he did it for the thrill of being able to. When the perennial school bully shows up wearing a 'kick me' sign, it's pretty hard to resist putting boot to butt.

But England had to work harder to prise Australia out in the second innings. Simon Jones, who took 5/44 in the first innings, suffered an ankle injury and could only bowl four overs. This opened the door for Ponting. He eased his way to 48, and Australia to 2/155, whittling the deficit down to 104. Such was the confidence of Australia at the time, they were eyeing a path to victory.

That's when Damien Martyn pushed the ball into the off side and called his captain through for a single. Ponting reacted quickly. But not as quickly as England substitute fielder Gary Pratt, who swooped in and hurled the stumps down. The throw found a ball-watching Ponting half a metre short of his ground.

Ponting's response to his dismissal was one of unfettered fury.

Since 1989, the Australians had held the Ashes by being better than England in every facet of the game – batting, bowling, captaining, sledging, keeping, not sending the opposition in to bat at the Gabba, catching and fielding. And leading the fielding excellence in that era had been Ponting himself. He, along with Mark Waugh, was among the best fielding fielders Australia had ever fielded on the field.

And here Ponting was, being run out by the exact same kind of outstanding fielding he'd inflicted on everybody else for so long. By some clown who wasn't even a Test cricketer. Who was on the ground substituting for an English bowler, as England had shamelessly done all series. A substitute fielding clown named 'Pratt', which was surely taking the piss now.

It would be enough to make anybody storm up the Trent Bridge pavilion steps hurling foul-mouthed accusations of cheating at Duncan Fletcher. Or, if not anybody, Ricky Ponting for sure.

Ponting had spoken to the match referee before the first Test about England's use of substitutes. In particular, what his camp perceived as England's tendency to rest bowlers after spells and bring on elite fielders as substitutes.

Australia's substitute fielder practices, in contrast, followed those used by all other nations. That substitute was their twelfth man, the player who'd just missed out on selection in the starting eleven.

A twelfth man was no more or less likely to be a great fielder than any of the regulars. As such, they tended to be substituted on only when there was genuine need. Substitute fielding was part of the general butlering duties assigned to the twelfth man. No more important than bringing out drinks, replacing gloves and bats, and other servile tasks. A fitting punishment for the player not good enough to make the starting team. That's what you get for dreaming, twelfthie!

Of course, sometimes the twelfth man happened to be an elite fielder. Most notably, the West Indies in the 1980s had called upon Roger Harper to perform terrific feats of athleticism. But Harper also often played for the West Indies, on the occasions where conditions virtually demanded they select a spinner. Gary Pratt wasn't ever going to be in the England starting side.

The 2005 England side weren't shy about pushing the limits of the laws of the game in their bid to regain the Ashes. As well as their substitution ploys, they later admitted to minor ball tampering. Saliva-augmenting Murray Mints gave them access to more reverse swing than they otherwise might have. The mints could helpfully be swallowed after they'd been used to illegally alter the ball's condition, leaving no evidence of their use. (A major advantage over using sandpaper – for the first time ever – in

South Africa, which was much harder to swallow.) Unlike the mints, Pratt remained very conspicuously on the field, accepting the plaudits of his teammates. Ponting grew more infuriated with each accepted backslap and high five.

Ponting's post-dismissal tantrum was dramatic. Unfortunately, however, it turned out that Pratt had every right to be on the field. Jones was genuinely injured. He would never play for England again.

Still, England's innovation of using the best fielder as substitute, even if they weren't within sight of the starting eleven, caught on. Australia soon adopted it too. Home Test squads would be augmented by the recruitment of a local promising youngster – such as baby David Warner or mini Marnus Labuschagne – renowned for their fielding talents.

This is perhaps fitting, since Ponting's frustrations with the entire concept of the twelfth man began when he was a mere promising youngster himself.

In the summer of 1994/95, with Zimbabwe and a far more inept England touring Australia, the traditional ODI tri-series had been augmented. It became a quadrangular status with the addition of an Australia A side containing the second tier of Australian players. Youngsters and fringe players such as Matthew Hayden, Damien Martyn, Justin Langer and a teenage Ricky Ponting.

It also contained a young Paul Reiffel, who proved to be a tidy and consistent bowler for Australia A throughout the preliminary rounds of the round-robin tournament. Tidy and consistent enough to help Australia A qualify for the finals against the full Australia side. Reiffel's reward for his efforts was to be 'promoted' from the Australia A squad to the main team – where he was then named as a tidy and consistent twelfth man for Australia. With this simple tactic, the senior team had negated one of Australia A's best bowlers. It was a piece of cricketing nonsense. The kind of thing that might have provided the first sparks of the young Ponting's suspicion of twelfth-man gamesmanship.

A dissatisfaction with twelfth men a decade in the making. No wonder Ponting flew off the handle over the Gary Pratt run-out. You can't hold that kind of anger in. It's not healthy.

NEXT:

Ricky Ponting may have lost his temper at his opponents. But at least he never tried to kick any of them. Plus, sculptor disappointment!

DENNIS LILLEE KICKS JAVED MIANDAD

Aggression

THE MOMENT:

In the first Test of the series between Australia and Pakistan in 1981/82, a fired-up Dennis Lillee kicks Javed Miandad, who threatens to retaliate with his bat

There are societal customs that we all more or less abide by, even if they aren't mandated by law. You don't walk into an elevator and face the back. You remove your AirPods before you head out on a date. You feign interest when a friend tells you they've started a true crime podcast.

Cricket has, over the centuries, developed its own societal customs. There are certain things that aren't done in polite cricketing society, even if no law explicitly prohibits them. It's like a lost Jane Austen novel – *Gully and Gullibility*, perhaps. ('Mr Darcy, until you can maintain a deferential line and length from the bowling crease, I suggest you shall never truly appreciate a maiden.' 'Oh, do shut up, Miss Bennett,' he said wittily, before unleashing a malicious bouncer that struck her square in the jaw.)

To push the boundaries of society's mores is to invite social ostracism. Or, at least, a lot of tut-tutting from the members' section.

Much of the tension between the Spirit of Cricket and the Laws of Cricket arises from this. It's a tension between these cricketing customs and the desire to win a match. The grey area where certain acts are allowed but there's some kind of social taboo that prevents them.

And the greyest of those grey areas is sledging. Interacting with your opponents is more or less an inevitable consequence of playing cricket. In its international formats, a cricket match can have anywhere between three and thirty hours of on-field play. That's a *long* time to give your opponents the silent treatment. Especially since at least half of that time is spent between deliveries, waiting for the next burst of action to begin.

One could, of course, always talk to your opponents in a positive fashion, applauding their shots, fashion and/or life choices. But as soon as there's a suspicion that it's possible to throw off an opponent's concentration with a piece of pithiness, and in the process gain an advantage in the match, somebody will almost always take the opportunity to do so.

Just about everybody agrees that the banter end of sledging is fine and the abuse end of sledging is rather less fine. Alas, almost nobody can agree on where the notorious line between these two extremes is. And mismatched opinions on the location of that line inevitably lead to friction.

What's more, since cricket is an international sport, played across a wide variety of very different cultures, it's easy for any comments to

be misinterpreted. One team's banter is another team's abuse. One team's gamesmanship is another team's cheating. One team's motivation is another team's niggle.

Javed Miandad niggled at an international level for more than twenty years. He began in his ODI debut in 1975 and continued through to his final ODI in 1996. His niggling drove opposition teams mad, because it operated on so many levels. For example, it's a well-known fact that Miandad was never given out LBW in Pakistan. So well-known is this fact that nobody cares that it's not true. Because it feels annoying enough to be right. (And, of course, the single most annoying thing about Miandad, from an opponent's perspective, was how consistently brilliant he was at batting. This was icing on an irritating cake. Carrot cake, one assumes, as it's the most irritating cake.)

Dennis Lillee had only played in six Tests against Miandad when the Pakistan batter comprehensively won the niggle battle.

Australia had bowled out Pakistan for 62 in the first innings of the match. This was in reply to Australia's first-innings score of 180. A second innings of 8/424 (declared) from Australia set up what would turn out to be an easy win. So on that front, Miandad's

Pakistan side were well behind. Yet on the niggle front, Miandad was about to put on a masterclass.

Despite having scored only 28 runs to that point, the Pakistan captain still somehow drove Lillee mental. To the point where the Australian fast bowler first bumped into him as part of his follow-through, then kicked Miandad as he made his ground.

There were no stump microphones or camera drones in 1981. So we have to rely on various biographies to try to glean how the situation had escalated to that point. Not surprisingly, versions bifurcate into two different tales.

Lillee blamed Miandad for the fashion in which the incident escalated. He claimed that his kick was merely a retaliation to Miandad shoving him. Greg Chappell invited further speculation about what the cameras might have missed by claiming Miandad's actions were 'the most disgraceful thing I have seen on a cricket pitch'.

Miandad's version lines up better with the television footage. He claims Lillee moved to get in his path as he completed his run. Miandad then pushed Lillee out of the road so he could make his ground.

But neither of the duelling retellings really matters. Whatever Miandad had done to drive Lillee to that point was conducted within the boundaries of polite cricketing society. (If not 'polite' society, then not at the extremes of 'impolite' society. Let's call it 'apolite' society.) Kicking a player in response to them annoying you, though, falls outside of the boundaries of polite, apolite and impolite cricketing society. It's also actually disallowed by the laws of the game. Cricket is not a contact sport (to the enormous frustration, no doubt, of Andrew Symonds).

The incident earned Lillee a two-match suspension. A minor victory for Miandad. (*Very* minor, considering the suspension covered two ODIs, one of which Pakistan didn't even compete in.) But better than nothing. In the ODI against Pakistan for which Lillee was suspended, Miandad was player of the match, scoring 72 from 82 deliveries to lead his team to victory. When Lillee returned in the second Test, he dismissed Miandad in both innings.

The moment is an iconic one in the history of Australia–Pakistan cricket. So much so that it would make sense for the two nations to play for a trophy named for it. After all, if you can't make a compelling trophy from the image of one man threatening to hit another man with a cricket bat after the second man kicked the first man in the bum, then, I'm sorry, you're a poor excuse for a sculptor.

We already have the Border–Gavaskar Trophy for series between Australia and India. And the Warne–Muralitharan Trophy for series between Australia and Sri Lanka. A Lillee–Miandad Trophy for series between Australia and Pakistan would be a fitting tribute not only to two great players, but also to the potential perils of having too much aggression in your cricket.

NEXT:

Bowlers shouldn't kick batters. They should instead vent their aggression via the leather projectile in their hand. Plus, Richard M Nixon!

HAROLD LARWOOD
HITS BERT OLDFIELD

Bodyline

THE MOMENT:

In the third Test of the 1932/33 Ashes, Harold Larwood of England, employing the bodyline tactics devised by Douglas Jardine, strikes Australian wicketkeeper Bert Oldfield in the head

One of the great things about sledging is that it's acquired such a bad reputation that Steve Waugh was convinced that 'mental disintegration' was a viable euphemism for it.

Think about that for a second. 'Oh no, what we're doing isn't something as awful as *sledging*. Goodness me, no. What we're doing is merely pulverising our opponents' minds. And doing so in such a fashion that all that remains of them is the scattered remnants of their constituent atomic particles.' Amazing.

As we've seen, there is a lot of grey area around mental disintegration. It can be difficult to determine what's harmless banter between two sides and what's something less harmless or banterful. There is, surprisingly, less grey area around attempts to *physically* disintegrate a player.

Every modern player is, sadly, well aware of exactly how lethal a cricket ball can be. Despite this, there are very few limits to how dangerous any delivery can be.

There are beamers, of course – balls that fly straight at the batter's head without first bouncing. These are considered beyond the pale, a violation of both the Laws and the Spirit of Cricket. Beamers are redeemed only by the fact that every bowler who bowls one can undo their malice with a simple apologetic wave of the hand. The wave makes clear the delivery was an accident. Marvellous to think that not a single beamer in the history of cricket has ever been deliberate.

It's not entirely clear why the beamer is singled out for such disapproval. The common argument is that it's so unexpected. Batters expect a ball to bounce somewhere on the pitch. A ball flying at their head without doing so is far more dangerous than a ball that flies at their head having first kissed the surface.

While this is true, it's still a little curious why defying the batter's expectations in this one specific instance is deemed unfair. Slower balls, wrong'uns and yorkers are also unexpected. They aren't considered unfair. But beamers are. It's not *crazy* to rule out a delivery so dangerous, but it's still an interesting quirk. And how much more interesting would cricket be if a beamer was a legal variation available to the bowling team, like a doosra or an over from Matthew Wade? Answer: *much* more interesting.

Apart from the beamer, however, there's no real Spirit of Cricket issue with targeting the batter's body or head. You can't do it too much, and the umpires will come down on you if you bowl more bouncers than legally allowed. But nobody will cast shame on you for the odd bouncer aimed at the head of a batter.

It wasn't always thus. In 1930, to the horror of all true Englishmen, young Donald Bradman had stormed his way through an Ashes tour. The lad scored 974 unstoppable runs at the preposterous average of 139.14. Bradman's Test average was 112.25 by the time the 1932/33 Ashes series rolled around. As far as new England captain Douglas Jardine was concerned, this wasn't big or clever. It was showing off. And something had to be done about it.

One of the more interesting cricket statistics is that Jardine has the highest Test average (applying the usual filter of at least twenty innings batted). But *only* if you exclude all the centuries. Presumably, Jardine's excellence *sans* centuries contributed to his hatred of Bradman's gaudy ton-making.

And so Jardine put a limit on Bradman's run-scoring antics in no uncertain terms. On the 1932/33 Ashes tour of Australia, he deployed bodyline, or, as it's more commonly known, fast leg theory. (The theory was that if you bowled the ball short and at the batter's body on a leg-stump line, with the leg-side field stacked with catchers, there was no real way for the batter to counter this.)

The tactic was a success in cricketing terms. England regained the Ashes. Bradman's average was more or less halved. And if other Australians succumbed to the short-pitched attack, led by Harold Larwood, then so be it. This all culminated in Bert Oldfield's skull being fractured by a Larwood short ball during the Adelaide Test. Australian captain Bill Woodfull's celebrated reaction was to claim 'there are two teams out there; one is trying to play cricket and the other is not'.

Jardine cared not one iota about the Australians' opinions on whether he was playing an acceptable form of cricket. He explained himself by pointing out: 'I've not travelled 6000 miles to make friends. I'm here to win the Ashes.' To his eternal credit, he was successful on both fronts.

Once the Ashes were secured for England, the Marylebone Cricket Club (MCC), the authorities in charge of the laws of the game, came around to Australia's way of thinking. They agreed that this kind of bowling was not on. The Laws of Cricket were clarified to prohibit such bowling in the future.

And that's pretty much been the pattern of short-pitched bowling ever since. Unlike some of the hazier Spirit of Cricket–based conventions of the game, what is or isn't allowed when it comes to bowling short has usually been swiftly enshrined in the laws of the game.

It's difficult to imagine that any bowler *actually* wants to harm a batter with the short ball. The goal of a bouncer is, in a way, not that much different from the goal of a sledge. By aiming *at* the head of a batter, the goal is to get *in* the head of a batter. To have them so wary of the danger of being injured that their ability to defend their wicket is hampered.

Larwood himself expressed this with perfect clarity. 'I never bowled to injure a man,' he said. 'Frighten them, intimidate them – yes.'

Sure, some bowlers may get carried away, posturing like professional wrestlers. Making claims that they want to see blood on the pitch or advising batters to get themselves out before they're forced to come around the wicket and kill them. But even that, one suspects, is theatre, designed to further intimidate the batter.

During the Vietnam War, President Richard Nixon attempted to use 'madman theory' to bring an end to the conflict. The basis of Nixon's theory was that if he could convince the North Vietnamese that he was crazy enough to use nuclear weapons, they'd have no choice but to negotiate terms of surrender.

It's very possible that posturing fast bowlers talking about how much they want to hurt batters are using their own version of madman theory. (Unleashing the odd beamer or two – definitely accidental – no doubt helps with this too.)

Ultimately, it all comes back to a variant of mental disintegration. To paraphrase two Australian cricket captains: 'There are two kinds of mental disintegration being employed in modern Test cricket; one is designed to convince the batter that the bowler is a madman, the other is not.'

NEXT:

It's not only the bowlers and fielders trying to get into the batters' heads. Sometimes the umpires have to do so too. Plus, Hollywood body-swap movies!

BEN STOKES

OBSTRUCTS THE FIELD

Mind Reading

THE MOMENT:

In a 2015 ODI, England batter Ben Stokes deflects a ball that bowler Mitchell Starc has hurled at the stumps after picking it up in his follow-through, and is given out for obstructing the field

Cricket often requires umpires to judge players not just by their actions but also by their intentions. Leg byes can only be counted if players are making a genuine attempt to play a shot or avoid the ball (or, in rarefied circumstances, both). Certain elements of the LBW law are also unlocked – like levels in a first-person shooter – if, in the umpire's opinion, no shot is being attempted.

This kind of telepathic adjudication is one of the more challenging aspects of being an umpire. Determining what a player *intended* to do requires mental powers that one might think are beyond most mortals.

But if you thought that, you'd be wrong. Because on social media, where people are always clear-eyed and free of any kinds of bias, there is, impressively, often great certainty about what a player must have been thinking at any given moment.

A Big Bash match in 2021 ended with Andrew Tye bowling a century-denying wide to James Vince. Straightaway, a knowing portion of social media gazed deep into Tye's heart. Their verdict? The wide was a deliberate dog act.

Of course, it may well have been. It's a possibility. But there are lots of wides in T20 cricket matches, as bowlers try their variations and get

them wrong. So it's also possible that Tye messed up a short ball. One can argue the various likelihoods of the two possibilities. But nobody other than Tye himself can ever know for sure what his intentions were.

It's not just Tye whose motivations social media users claim to understand with unshakeable clarity. Any aspect of cricket that requires an assessment of what a player intended to do will generate a torrent of certainty about the player's intentions. That torrent will make clear why their behaviour was either reprehensible or comprehensible.

Unsurprisingly, the certainty that social media denizens have for a player's motives almost always align with whether the player is a member of the team that they support. And that was never truer than in the second ODI between England and Australia in 2015.

Mitchell Starc had bowled a full ball that Ben Stokes had defended straight back down the pitch. In the process, however, he'd taken a couple of steps outside his crease. Starc, who had gathered the ball in his follow-through, therefore threw the ball at the batter's stumps. Stokes recoiled away from the incoming ball, but also stuck out his left hand and deflected it away, while still out of his ground.

The Australians appealed. The on-field umpires sent it upstairs. The third umpire assessed the situation and decreed that Stokes was out. He was the first Englishman ever to be given out for obstructing the field in a one-day international.

The key question was whether Stokes had *wilfully* deflected the ball, or whether he'd *instinctively* done so. Opinions on the matter split straight down national lines.

The argument from England fans was that Stokes was trying to avoid being hit. He couldn't possibly have had time to deliberately parry the ball away to avoid being run out.

The counter from Australian fans was simple. Stokes had, less than a month earlier, taken a split-second slips catch as part of Australia's horrid Trent Bridge 60 all out, which showcased his incredible reaction time. Was it so implausible that he could throw out his hand to block a cricket ball that was heading for his stumps?

Besides, should it matter if Stokes's actions were instinctive or wilful? Batters do a lot of things instinctively. Why, against Mitchell Starc alone, many batters over the years had instinctively avoided his toe-crushing yorkers, allowing the ball to hit the stumps. Should proper cricket etiquette have required such batters to be

called back immediately, because they were trying to avoid being injured and reacted instinctively?

That prospect is raised because the argument among fans and commentators was not only whether Stokes should have been given out. There were also arguments about whether Australian captain Steve Smith had violated the Spirit of Cricket. Arguments that claimed he should have withdrawn his appeal and allowed Stokes to bat on.

Now we see the power of the Spirit of Cricket. A naive newcomer to the sport might understand the idea of a set of guidelines that *augmented* the laws of the game. An ethical approach that provided examples of actions that, while technically permissible, were frowned upon.

But the Spirit of Cricket is more complicated than that. It doesn't merely augment. It actively *defies* the laws in instances such as this. According to some Spirit of Cricket adherents, the Australians had misbehaved by asking if a batter was out. And then compounded it by accepting the decision of the umpire.

This is wild stuff, yet after the match England captain Eoin Morgan ran with it. With a straight face, Morgan suggested he would have retracted the appeal for Stokes's legal dismissal. On one hand, not a surprise. England were chasing 310 from 49 overs and Stokes was one of their key batters. Calling Stokes back after he'd been given out would have been just the thing Morgan needed to bolster his team's chances.

But no, of course Morgan wasn't referring to him being allowed to call one of his own dismissed batters back to the crease. He instead meant that if he'd somehow been captain of Australia, as a result of, say, some kind of Hollywood body-swapping movie plot device, then, in that wacky, high-concept box-office-smashing blockbuster comedy scenario, he would have recalled Stokes.

Perhaps Smith could have used Morgan's position as a negotiating point. Agree with Morgan that he'd retract all future 'obstructing the field' appeals. But only on the condition that England also recalled all players caught at, say, first slip?

While this is ridiculous, it's not immediately clear what the difference is. And yet the Spirit of Cricket, as interpreted by most English fans at the time (and, to be fair, also by noted non-English New Zealand captain and Spirit of Cricket enthusiast Brendon McCullum), was clear on the matter. They'd divined Stokes's motivations for his actions. He'd been deemed

to be pure of heart. Therefore, all wrongdoing for the moment had to be shifted to the nefarious Australians.

This kind of Spirit of Cricket jujitsu was acceptable, because the Australians' motives were as easily inferred as Stokes's. You barely even needed any mind-reading abilities at all to understand what drove them. They wanted to win the game, and were willing to stop at nothing to do so.

Even if that meant, um, playing by the rules.

NEXT:

Australia continue to play by the rules. But this time in such an underhanded way that everybody agrees it violates the Spirit of Cricket. Plus, distracted boyfriends!

TREVOR CHAPPELL
BOWLS AN UNDERARM DELIVERY

Underarm

THE MOMENT:

In 1981, with one ball of the final over remaining in an ODI final, Greg Chappell instructs his brother Trevor to bowl underarm to prevent New Zealand from hitting a six to tie the match

There was no social media for the underarm incident in 1981. This is a shame, because it would have been ripe fodder for assorted memes.

It's simple enough to imagine a Milkshake Duck–like response. 'The whole internet loves Greg Chappell, a lovely Australian captain who captains Australia! *1 underarm delivery later* We regret to inform you Chappell is unsportsmanlike.'

Or the creation of a parody account called @TrevsUnderarmBall, saying things like 'Don't stop me now! I'm on a roll!!!'.

Or a distracted boyfriend meme, with the boyfriend being labelled 'cricket media', the hot girl in the red dress labelled 'New Zealand outrage' and the current girlfriend being 'Greg Chappell's outstanding lateral thinking, which exploited his peerless under-standing of the playing conditions'.

It's the last of these that would have had the most punch. Because even today there's not enough credit given to Greg Chappell's out-of-the-box thinking.

Chappell was mentally exhausted. He was dealing with the pressure of the match situation. He was also desperate to win the match to avoid the finals series from going one match longer than it needed to. Given this, his ability to innovate on the spot was,

from a non–Spirit of Cricket perspec-tive, brilliant.

He knew the playing conditions and the history of the sport well. So well, in fact, that he was able to combine them in a pressure moment to ensure victory when a lesser captain would have settled for risking a tie.

If playing by the rules was valued above adhering to the Spirit of Cricket, there'd be only one player attracting criticism after the match. That would have been New Zealand batter Brian McKechnie, who would have been fined for tossing his bat away after the delivery was rolled to him.

But, of course, McKechnie's disappointment wasn't where the media storm landed after the match ended. No, the hurricane of disgust landed instead on the head of Greg Chappell.

And if there had been social media in 1981, it seems unlikely that it would have split along the usual partisan lines. Pretty much *everybody* agrees that Chappell's decision to order an underarm delivery was a wrong one, even though it was within the Laws of Cricket at the time. (This was changed swiftly thereafter. Yet another indicator of the instant disdain with which the ploy was viewed.)

Heck, even Chappell himself acknowledges, in hindsight, that

ordering the underarm was the wrong thing to do.

The key to why everybody in cricket is united on this front is summarised by New Zealand Prime Minister Robert Muldoon's tweetable zinger: 'It was an act of cowardice and I consider it appropriate that the Australian team were wearing yellow.'

Cricket is, at its heart, a one-on-one confrontation between bat and ball. One player runs in and bowls. An opposition player then attempts to negotiate that delivery. From there, all else follows. Fielders get involved. Runs are contemplated and scored. Umpires summon forth specific hand gestures to indicate the result.

It's a battle of great skill (the batting of Josh Hazlewood notwithstanding). Any cricketer of international standard needs to revel in such battles. After all, they're competing in hours and hours of them every time they play. Furthermore, to have reached the international level of cricket, those same players must also have taken part in countless training sessions over their lives to hone their skills for these confrontations.

Chappell effectively sidestepped that entire bat and ball battle. And, ultimately, the avoidance of that fundamental cricketing face-off is what summoned the fearsome ire of the Spirit of Cricket.

The Spirit of Cricket is a conservative force. It's a counter to players searching for loopholes within the laws and the playing conditions – an overriding set of guidelines that aim to ensure the sport is about that contest between bat and ball.

Bodyline was deemed a violation because, in a helmetless era, it moved the focus of a batter to survival, rather than enabling a proper athletic contest. Like underarm, it was within the laws at the time, before swiftly becoming not so, because of its violation of the Spirit of Cricket.

Sometimes the Spirit of Cricket is *too* conservative. It once frowned upon such worthy innovations as the wrong'un (known at the time as 'the Bosey') as being unfair. It also tends to make people suspicious of legal dismissals such as 'obstructing the field' simply because they're uncommon.

But there's a balance. Players, captains and coaches strive for innovation. The Spirit of Cricket pulls everything back to the bowler–batter confrontation. This balance is fundamental to the evolution of cricket.

In the book *A New Kind of Science*, renowned mathematician Stephen Wolfram explained the results of his analysis of cellular automata. The details of his analysis aren't worth delving into here, but his conclusions are surprisingly relevant to cricket.

Wolfram showed that sets of rules can be classified into four different types. (The rules can be any kind of rules. They can be logic circuits in computers. Or neurons firing in brain cells. Or neural network circuits firing in computerised brain cells. Anything.) Wolfram originally considered rules for turning lights on and off. Because that's the kind of thrillseekers mathematicians tend to be.

Rule classes 1 and 2 are cases where the rules lead to either static or repetitive outcomes. Class 3 is the case where the outcome of the rules is effectively random or unpredictable.

None of the first three classes of rules is particularly interesting. Things are either too predictable or too chaotic.

But Wolfram's Class 4 is the Goldilocks case. This is the sets of rules where, in Wolfram's words, there's 'a mixture of order and randomness: localised structures are produced which on their own are fairly simple, but these structures move around and interact with each other in very complicated ways'.

Class 4 rules are fundamental to chaos theory. Indeed, they're often described as being 'the edge of chaos'. But they're also fundamental to the theory of evolution, and to life itself. If genetic mutation is too random, offspring die off immediately. Life withers away. If genetic mutation is too slow, a species can't adapt to its environment. Intelligent life exists because of Class 4 rules (in this case, the biological foundations of DNA). Those rules balance both a force of innovation and a force of conservatism against one another.

In cricket, there's a similar balance. This allows the sport to evolve and innovate, introducing different formats along the way to keep it relevant to the changing needs of fans. All while still remaining, at its core, a sport that celebrates the same fundamental set of electrifying athletic skills.

The Laws of Cricket define the sport, allowing cricketers to show off the skills of the game. But in situations where the laws are flawed, they're bolstered by an overriding conservative evolutionary counterforce that brings the sport to a Wolframesque Class 4 equilibrium.

Probably wise to call that the Spirit of Cricket for short.

NEXT:

This would be a good place to wrap up the Spirit of Cricket – were it not for the one law that conflicts with it, and which can't be changed. Plus, brainwashed cultists!

VINOO MANKAD
RUNS OUT BILL BROWN

Mankads

THE MOMENT:

In the second Test of the 1947/48 series between Australia and India, bowler Vinoo Mankad runs out Bill Brown for backing up too far

In the Laws of Cricket, there is a preamble which refers specifically to the Spirit of Cricket. 'Cricket owes much of its appeal and enjoyment to the fact that it should be played not only according to the Laws, but also within the Spirit of Cricket,' this preamble asserts.

As we've seen, the Spirit of Cricket works as a failsafe for the laws. The laws may have loopholes that allow players to sidestep the bat-and-ball confrontation that lies at the heart of cricket. If so, the Spirit of Cricket flies in to wag its spectral finger at the players doing the sidestepping.

Once detected, those loophole laws are usually rectified. But there's one law that the Spirit of Cricket *hates*, but which can't be changed. Because it's fundamental to the sport.

I refer, of course, to the mankad.

The mankad is, conceptually, a simple form of dismissal. If the non-striker is outside their crease as the bowler comes in to bowl, that bowler can run them out before delivering the ball. Easy-peasy. Yet this simple method of executing a run-out infuriates a not insignificant number of people. Those people refuse to see it as anything other than a gross violation of the Spirit of Cricket.

These mankad adversaries ('mankadversaries' for short) are everywhere. So much so that some members of the Mankad family have requested that the dismissal not be referred to by that name. Their argument being that it tarnishes the legacy of Vinoo Mankad, who was a magnificent all-rounder by any measure.

This is sad, on many levels. Firstly, because it's a request to remove a magnificent term from the game. Yes, a mankad is just a form of run-out. But it's such a specific kind that it's convenient to have a shorthand. So why not one that celebrates the bowler who most memorably wielded it?

But secondly, it's wrongheaded to think that the term *mankad* denigrates Mankad himself, when there's nothing wrong with a mankad.

(Having said that, you've probably noticed that I'm using mankad with a lower case 'm' for the dismissal to help distinguish it from the player. Such usage also suggests that the term has transcended Mankad himself, which also feels accurate.)

In fact, not only is there nothing wrong with a mankad, a moment's thought should make clear that it's a *completely necessary* form of dismissal in the game.

Without the prospect of a mankad, non-strikers could stand

wherever they like, with no fear of repercussion. Indeed, of all the mad things the New Zealand team did in the tied 2019 World Cup final, not starting every ball of the Super Over halfway down the pitch was among the maddest. England had injected the Spirit of Cricket into their veins. They had gone on record saying they'd never mankad anybody. This should have given New Zealand the opportunity to gain crucial extra metres on every desperate run.

Yet they didn't. Perhaps they were aware that many mankadversaries will sometimes swallow their umbrage and contemplate a mankad. But only if the non-striker is thought to be 'taking the piss'. That is, if they're standing *too* far out of their ground.

The definition of 'too far' here, and how it differs from the normal absent-minded drifting out of one's crease, can, however, be vague. For clarity's sake, there needs to be some kind of line marked on the pitch to designate this threshold, behind which a non-striker should stay.

So a mankadversary may be willing to contemplate a mankad for a repeat, piss-taking offender. But even so, there is one more hurdle to overcome. The offender needs to be warned. This is considered to be the 'right' way to go about a mankad. To mankad someone without a warning is yet another Spirit of Cricket violation.

This too is nonsense. Wicketkeepers don't give warnings before completing a stumping. Bowlers don't give heads-ups about upcoming yorkers that may well shatter the stumps. And not once did Ricky Ponting swoop in from cover to gather a ball, then pause to warn the foolish batters trying to take a quick single that if they did it again, he'd throw the stumps down.

Every objection to mankads can be swatted away with the tiniest amount of logical thought. Yet mankadversaries will still cling to their irrational beliefs, like a brainwashed cultist or a 45th President of the United States. 'I just don't like them,' they will claim. 'It's a bad look.'

Which would mostly elicit befuddled shrugs. Except for the fact that, maddeningly, almost every professional cricketer agrees. Not just batters prone to drifting out of their crease either. Bowlers too.

In 2020, Glenn McGrath was asked the following question:

'It's the World Cup final and you have the last wicket to get. The opposition needs two runs to win. Would you consider mankading?'

His response was one word: 'No.'

And, okay. Fair enough for McGrath, who figures that with two entire runs up his sleeve he can add a bonus wicket to his record. Better for him to claim it than lose it to the netherworld of the unattributed run-out.

But for pretty much everybody else, this is *insane*. It's a run-out, for goodness sake.

This hatred of the mankad by professional players aligns with the Spirit of Cricket. No law avoids the contest between bowler and batter more than the mankad.

Worse, any damn fool could do it. No cricketing skill required.

For fans of the game with no delusions about their prospects for competing at an international standard, then, mankads are a bit of fun. A delightful diversion. A careless batter has wandered out of their crease and received their delicious comeuppance. Ha, ha, ha. Take that, you inattentive dummy.

For top-level cricketers, however, a mankad must feel like an existential threat. A form of dismissal that requires no skill, and which is impossible to counter. (Oops. Sorry. Which is *trivial* to counter. That's 'trivial', not 'impossible'.)

The key, then, to rehabilitating mankads in the eyes of the players is to appeal not to something as tedious as logic and rational arguments. Instead, we need to make mankads competitive. Fortunately, there's a way that can be done.

In 2013, the Laws of Cricket were changed so that a no ball would be called if a bowler hit the non-striker's end stumps during their delivery stride. This was in response to England bowler Steven Finn, who did this all the time – to the extent that South African captain Graeme Smith began complaining that he was being distracted by Finn's oafishness.

The Finn no ball is the key to mankad acceptability. As the mankad currently stands, there is no risk to the bowler. Any time they like, they can attempt a mankad with no penalty against them if the non-striker is inside their crease.

But if the laws were to be expanded to make a failed mankad a Finn no ball, then now we have a contest. Imagine non-strikers inching further and further out of their crease, tempting the bowler to mankad them, yet always prepared to dive back into their ground, as they try to earn their side a no ball (and, in white-ball cricket, a free hit for their batting partner). It works for baseball with stealing bases. Cricket shouldn't be too proud to borrow a similar idea.

Will you be mankaded by the bowler? Or will you finn them instead? That's a challenge worthy of an international cricketer.

NEXT:

The Laws and Spirit of Cricket provide structure for players and administrators. Within that structure, we see the evolution of cricket. Plus, taped VHS highlights!

THE EVOLUTION OF CRICKET

MICHAEL BEVAN

BEVAN

HITS A FOUR

Final-ball Finishes

THE MOMENT:

On New Year's Day 1996, with one ball
remaining in an ODI against the West
Indies, Michael Bevan hits Roger Harper
straight down the ground for the match-
winning four

It's one of the most celebrated moments in the history of Australian cricket. It took place in Sydney on the first day of 1996, in the fifth match of the annual ODI tri-series. Michael Bevan helped Australia recover from 6/38, chasing 173 for victory in a rain-reduced match.

Bevan kept the kind of cool head that the rest of the batters had lacked. He whittled down the run chase with a combination of sharp singles and per-fectly judged twos. Whenever the run rate threatened to get out of control, he would throw a boundary into the mix.

Partnering with Ian Healy, player of the match Paul Reiffel, Shane Warne and, finally, Glenn McGrath, Bevan guided Australia unerringly towards the target. Until, finally, the match reduced to one simple equation. If he could hit the final ball of the match for four runs, Australia would win. If he couldn't, then the West Indies would win.

This is the ideal finish to any cricket match. A match that goes down to the final ball is the most thrilling possible outcome. (I mean, *all* matches finish on the final ball. That's what 'final' means. But we're talking about when there are different results still realistically available on the final ball. You knew that. Stop being so pedantic.)

With Test matches, it doesn't even have to be the final ball. Merely enter-ing the final session of the match with at least a pair of results still possible is gripping enough.

This is not only because Test matches are afforded greater importance and gravitas than their limited-overs counterparts. It's also because Test matches are longer. Having already put more than four days of effort into a Test, a match that can still be won, lost, drawn or even tied as it heads into its final hours increases the pressure on the players.

In a variation of the sunk cost fallacy, players are wary of making any mistakes in those final clutch moments. Any blunders that would undo the previous four days of work. Because while tight finishes are fabulous for fans to watch, they're antithetical to the goals of players. Cricketers may enjoy the adrenaline of the closeness of the contest. They may also acknowledge its appeal as an athlete. But a match that goes down to the wire is, by definition, one that's more easily lost by a single error. An optimised cricketer looking to maximise their victories would logically look to *minimise* the number of finishes where a simple misstep can lead to a non-incrementation of that victory counter.

Which brings the cricketers into conflict with the fans – and, hence, with the administrators too. The latter *want* close finishes and will push the game in directions to make them more likely. Most of the innovations in limited-overs cricket were designed to make final-ball finishes where either team can win more likely.

The tension built up over five days is eliminated from a one-day match. But the removal of the draw as an outcome ensures that the team batting second never gives up on the chase. Limiting the number of overs a player can bowl also serves to make the sides more equal, again increasing the chances of a tight finish. Flatter, more consistent pitches, designed to aid batting, also help. They ensure conditions are as similar as possible for both teams.

(The T20 format stretches these principles still further. The shorter the game, the more likely it is to have a tight finish.)

A shorter match has less riding on it than a longer match. But from the perspective of most fans (and admin-istrators), the increased chance of a last-ball finish makes this a worthwhile trade-off. So when Bevan got Australia to a position where a four from the final ball of the match would win it, this was the dream conclusion to the match.

Roger Harper was the bowler. Earlier in the innings, he'd dropped a caught-and-bowled chance from Bevan. (He'd excitedly claimed the catch at the time. Let's generously assume that Harper thought it had dropped from his hands and lodged between his legs without hitting the ground at any point.) Now was his chance to redeem himself. He'd bowled a dot ball from the second-last ball of the match. Anything even close to resembling that delivery, full and angled in, would be enough for the West Indies.

Instead, the ball was pitched shorter, allowing Bevan to step away and thump it straight. The ball flew over the umpire's head and down the ground, thudding into the boundary fence below the sightscreen. It was one of the great shots in the history of Australian cricket, making Bevan an instant hero for fans of the game.

And nobody in Sydney saw it.

I mean, that's not quite true, obviously. There was an official crowd of 37,562 at the game. Some would have left during the rain that had seen the match reduced to 43 overs a side. Others would have given up and gone home after Australia's early collapse. But there may still have been as many as 30,000 losing their minds as Bevan drilled his match-winning shot straight down the ground.

But that 30,000 was less than 1 per cent of Sydney's population in 1996. And none of the other 99 per cent had any way of watching Bevan's heroics. The match was a sellout. The general public tickets for the match would have been snapped up well in advance, as was always the case for Australia v West Indies ODIs of that era. Any shortfall in capacity crowd numbers could be attributed to rain-wary SCG members. Despite there being no more tickets available, the television coverage was still blacked out in the home city, as per tradition.

And so Sydneysiders who wanted to follow the run chase had to do so via radio. And if they wanted to see it, they'd have to wait for the official highlights broadcast later in the evening. On the plus side, they could record those highlights onto VHS tape, and then watch them over and over until YouTube was invented.

Bevan's four changed not just the perceptions of what was possible in a run chase. It also changed the perceptions of what was possible in cricketing broadcasts. For such an ideal conclusion to a game of cricket to be denied to 99 per cent of the nation's biggest market of cricket fans seemed preposterous. And so, shortly after, in the tri-series finals between Australia and Sri Lanka later that summer, the ACB allowed Channel Nine to broadcast the match into the home city if it was sold out. (A decade later, even the sellout restriction was lifted.)

After all, there's no point in having the perfect finish to a match if people aren't able to see it.

NEXT:

Letting fans in the host city watch the cricket on television is one way to expand its audience. Another way is to double the number of teams by supporting women's cricket. Plus, crime-solving dolphins!

ALYSSA HEALY

COMPLETES A RUN-OUT

The Women's Big Bash League

THE MOMENT:

In 2019, the second semi-final of WBBL04 looks certain to be won from the final ball by the Melbourne Renegades, before precision fielding from the Sydney Sixers sends the match into a Super Over

For a long time, women were invisible in cricket. Much like Sue 'Invisible Woman' Storm of the Fantastic Four. But unlike Sue, not in a way that allowed them to get into rollicking adventures against such foes as Dr Doom, Galactus or the Super-Skrull.

It was possible to be a devoted cricket fan for decades and yet have seen only the tiniest proportion of women's cricket. A highlights reel of a World Cup win, perhaps, delivered as a curiosity somewhere in the sports section of the nightly news. Not at the top of the news, obviously. But maybe after reports of a footballer having knee reconstruction surgery that's ruled him out for the rest of the season. Or a puff piece about an Olympic swimmer releasing a children's book about a crime-solving dolphin.

In Australia, that began to change with the introduction of the Women's Big Bash League. A generation of some of Australia's finest women cricketers had emerged. By dint of their excellence, they managed to poke their heads out of the invisibility well in which female athletes had traditionally resided. To Cricket Australia's credit, they built on that. They expanded the BBL competition, which had been men only for the first four years, creating a separate women's competition from 2015/16. And to the women's credit, they delivered cricket so entertaining that they forced their way onto television coverage by sheer watchability.

The watchability highlight of the WBBL came in the semi-finals of the 2018/19 season.

In the first semi-final, the Sydney Thunder's Nicola Carey needed four off the final ball to tie the match and send it to a Super Over. Brisbane Heat bowler Jess Jonassen had bowled during the six-over Power Play at the start of the innings. She'd been carted for 23 off two overs. But now she was back, bowling the final over.

Jonassen's first five balls were tidy, with four singles and just the one boundary. Her sixth and final ball, however, was in the slot for Carey. She went down on one knee and lofted it out towards the square leg boundary. She struck it long and high towards the rope. A four would tie the match. A six would win it.

Or, alternatively, Haidee Birkett racing around the boundary's edge could take a one-handed catch at full speed to win it for the Heat. Jonassen, who had crouched down in despair as Carey struck her shot, leapt up in celebration. It was a remarkable finish to a remarkable semi-final.

The second-most remarkable of the day, as it would turn out.

Because in the second semi-final, the Melbourne Renegades got within three runs of victory with one ball remaining. The match had again gone down to the final ball. This time, with Sophie Molineux facing up to Sydney Sixers bowler Ellyse Perry.

Perry would go on to win Player of the Tournament. For her batting exploits on this occasion. She would end the competition with 777 runs at an average of 86.33 and a strike rate of 121.21. Earlier in the day, opening the batting, she'd top-scored with 54 not out from 59 balls to anchor the Sixers' 4/131 from their 20 overs.

But Perry was, of course, still an experienced and skilful death bowler. So Molineux, who opened for the Renegades and who was one run behind Perry's score for the Sixers with one ball remaining, had her work cut out for her.

Perry, bowling right arm over the wicket, angled it across the left-handed Molineux. She swung hard, slicing it over the backward point fielder. The ball flew towards the rope for the match-winning boundary. However, sprinting around in the deep was Erin Burns. Despite Burns's desperate strides, the ball looked certain to reach the rope first. But Burns dived at full-length, swatting at the ball

with her outstretched right arm. She flicked it away, mere centimetres from the boundary.

While all this was going on, Molineux and non-striker Claire Koski were charging between the wickets. The boundary would have secured them victory, but it was more than they needed. Three runs would suffice. By the time the Sixers' Sarah Aley came around from fine leg to recover Burns's desperate save, they'd completed two of them.

Koski, the non-striker who'd had the head start on the running, was already halfway back for the third. By the time Aley's flat, hard throw came in from the deep to wicketkeeper Alyssa Healy, she had made her ground for the match-winning run. Molineux, however, was only halfway through her portion of it.

Healy took the throw a pace and a half away from the stumps at her end, and in one action pirouetted and threw at the non-striker's end. Perry had retreated back to the stumps at the bowler's end, but saw that the aim of Healy's split-second throw was true. Molineux emulated Burns's dive, stretching out her bat in a desperate attempt to secure her side a spot in the final. Perry, meanwhile, resisted any urge to intercept Healy's throw and allowed it to crash into middle stump.

There would be a replay to check, but nobody on the ground other than the umpire needed it. It was a sensational piece of three-person fielding that required speed, determination and precision. The Sydney Sixers had pulled off an unbelievable run-out to send the semi-final into a Super Over. A Super Over they inevitably won.

If there had been any doubt about whether the WBBL still needed double-headers with the men to prove its worth, those doubts were gone. The women could do brilliant, hair-raising double-headers perfectly well on their own, thanks very much.

From the following season, the WBBL would be its own tournament, played in its own window, separate from the men.

A little over a year later, Jonassen, Carey, Molineux and Healy would all play at the MCG in the women's T20 World Cup final, in front of a record women's cricket crowd of 86,174. Perry, injured earlier in the tournament, would join fellow squad member Burns, watching from the dugout.

It was an elite Australian squad, hardened still further by competing in the toughest women's tournament in the world. As a result, the T20 World Cup final would not get anywhere near the last ball.

NEXT:

Did you know that men also play T20 cricket? Some of them to a standard high enough to earn them very large amounts of money. Plus, mandatory Spotify playlists!

GLENN MAXWELL

SCORES A MILLION-DOLLAR GOLDEN DUCK

T20 Tournaments

THE MOMENT:

Glenn Maxwell's disappointment at scoring a golden duck in the second ODI against the West Indies in 2013 is tempered by the Mumbai Indians simultaneously paying a million US dollars for him at the IPL auction

It was an otherwise unspectacular ODI in an otherwise unspectacular summer. Australia batted first and lost wickets in pairs early on. Openers Aaron Finch and Usman Khawaja were both out within the first eight overs to leave the score at 2/25. Phillip Hughes and captain Michael Clarke both fell with the score on 56. Then Matthew Wade and Glenn Maxwell fell within five balls of one another, leaving Australia 6/98 halfway through their innings.

Maxwell returned to the dressing room, where coach Mickey Arthur and Clarke pulled him aside. But the criticism he expected for his first-ball duck, bowled by Darren Sammy, never came. Instead, captain and coach revealed to the 24-year-old that he was now a millionaire. The bidding at the IPL auction that was taking place at the same time had gone well beyond the US$200,000 base price that Maxwell had set.

The Mumbai Indians had paid a million US dollars for him, making him the most expensive purchase of the auction.

Maxwell returned to the field in the second innings to help defend Australia's total of 7/266 – the innings had been rescued by a George Bailey century. Emboldened by the IPL show of faith, Maxwell took 4/63 from 8.1 overs with his off-spin. The West Indies were bowled out for 212 in the 39th over.

If Maxwell's bowling figures suggested he was buying wickets, who could blame him? He was a millionaire now. What did he care?

The Maxwell millions weren't unprecedented for Australians in the IPL. A couple of years earlier, David Hussey (US$1.4 million) and Cameron White (US$1.1 million) both broke the million-dollar barrier. Andrew Symonds had earned US$1.35 million in the very first IPL auction. But those players had all finished their international careers. Their abilities were known and the IPL served as a welcome superannuation scheme. Maxwell was only eight ODIs and nine T20Is into his international career. This wasn't retirement money. It was a down-payment on his potential.

Maxwell had already established himself as a free-scoring, risk-taking, shot-inventing whirligig. He was equally likely to frustrate or exhilarate, augmenting every cricket match in which he played with his frenetic brand of Maxwellball.

The million-dollar gamble on Maxwell was emblematic of the power of the IPL. No other nation could compete with India's wealth. (Indeed, the riches on offer would further hasten the demise of the West Indies as a Test cricket force. Many of their most promising new players began to eschew the longest format. Understandably, they preferred to instead secure their futures with the T20 franchise wealth available.)

Other T20 tournaments couldn't compete with the IPL in monetary terms. But the circular economics of a domestic T20 league pushed administrators down predictable paths. Interest in a T20 tournament begets television ratings. Television ratings beget advertising dollars. Advertising dollars beget more money going into the tournament. More tournament money begets more money being available with which to pay players. More pay for players begets the best players in the world competing. The best players in the world competing begets further interest in the tournament. Repeat ad(vertising) infinitum.

The economics of T20 tournaments are a virtuous circle when they work, and a vicious one when they don't. The easiest way of kick-starting the process – or, if not the easiest, then the cheapest – is by tweaking the rules of the competition. If new rules generate tournament interest, then you're away. And that has been the standard approach of administrators over the years.

Australia's Big Bash tournament organisers cleverly played their biggest card early. They expanded out of their boring old single-sex BBL tournament with the addition of the WBBL in 2015. This was not only a savvy marketing tactic, it was also a success from the perspective of social equity. Something that perhaps can't be said for the introduction of Power Surges, Bash Boosts and X-Factors in the 2020/21 season.

The Caribbean Premier League has tinkered less with the rules. They provided net-run-rate penalties for slow over rates and permitted one (1) team to call themselves the 'St Lucia Zouks'.

The Bangladesh Premier League, on the other hand, made it mandatory for teams to have bowlers who bowled leg-spin and faster than 140 kilometres per hour. (Two separate bowlers, to be clear, although presumably a 140 kilometres-per-hour leg-spinner, if available, would be selected in a flash.)

And, of course, the New Zealand Super Smash required all players to subscribe to a Dave Dobbyn Spotify playlist.

But these efforts all pale into comparison with the work of England and South Africa. Those two nations have responded to the desperate search for eyeballs by tearing up the T20 format completely.

England came up with The Hundred, in which instead of the 120 balls that are traditional in 20 overs of cricket, teams would bowl a handily decimalised 100 deliveries.

If you've observed that 100 isn't divisible by six, then you've spotted the basis for most of the other rule changes involved in The Hundred. Bowlers bowl overs of five balls each. Or sometimes ten balls. But no more than twenty per match. Bowling ends are only changed every ten balls. Also, everybody is dressed as a packet of crisps. (Fun fact: not one single rule here has been invented for comedic purposes.)

South Africa, meanwhile, went one step better. Cricket South Africa tinkered not at the edges, like the hesitant cowards of other nations. No, CSA tossed away the tinkerer's scalpel of earlier eras and replaced it with a modern-day lumberjack's axe. With it, they hacked away at the most fundamental premise of the sport: that cricket should be a competition between a mere *two* teams.

Three team cricket (3TC) was a revelation. Hill fishermen catching sixes in COVID-safe nets. A tournament sponsored by rain (actually Rain, a mobile data company, but still . . .). Makhaya Ntini on commentary

guffawing at the antics of his son. Everything about it was amazing.

It's impossible to tell how the shorter forms of cricket will evolve in the future. T20 cricket and their variants are the Petri dishes of the sport, pushing it to evolve with maximum rapidity. Maxwell and others of his ilk are the catalysts, effortlessly providing the quick thrills that draw the audiences so crucial for tournament success.

Heck, even Maxwell's golden ducks generate buzz all around the world. Such as in BBL04, when he left an in-swinging delivery that smashed straight into his stumps.

If that kind of social media viral marketing isn't worth a million dollars, what is?

NEXT:

T20 cricket and its variants help evolve the modern game. Earlier evolution was simpler, with even coloured clothing considered a breakthrough. Plus, I Dream of Jeannie!

KERRY PACKER ORDERS COLOURED CLOTHING

Colours

THE MOMENT:

In the final preliminary match of the 1978/79 limited-overs International Cup in World Series Cricket, WSC Australia and WSC West Indies both take the field in coloured clothing

In March 1975, television stations in Australia began broadcasting in colour for the first time. Gone was the monochrome black-and-whiteness to which 1970s television viewers had become accustomed. In its place, a dizzying spectrum of all manner of hues.

The United States had made the transition from black and white to colour several years earlier. Shows such as *I Dream of Jeannie* (featuring a magic-wielding, midriff-exposing Barbara Eden) and *Lost in Space* (featuring a danger-decreeing, arm-flailing robot) both made the switch between seasons.

By 1979, in Australia, it was time for cricket to embrace a similar sense of both magic and danger as it made the transition to colour.

Kerry Packer's World Series Cricket had made several innovations over its first year of existence. The most notable one had been the introduction of day-night cricket. (Well, most notable on-field innovation, that is. The most notable off-field innovation was the one where they secretly signed up all the good players in the world to play in their rebel tournament, to the horror of cricket boards everywhere. Helluva innovation, that one.)

The day-night matches required the introduction of a white ball. This was because the red ball became too difficult to see under lights. But a white ball came with its own problems. The major one being that it was harder to see against the traditional white kit of the players.

The obvious solution was to change the colours that the players wore. However, it took until late in the second summer of World Series Cricket before this solution was implemented. And on 17 January 1979, cricket – as predicted by the traditionalists throughout the entire Packer confrontation – finally dyed.

On that day, the WSC West Indies side (hereafter, just 'West Indies') and WSC Australia (again, 'Australia' is fine) strode onto the SCG, sporting coloured garb. The boring old whites that had dominated cricket since its start had been discarded in dramatic fashion. And there were few fashions more dramatic than the West Indies' kits of startling pink.

There would be no turning back from this point. Cricket was reunited the following year. Day-night ODIs became the preferred brand of summer entertainment. And with those day-night ODIs came colourful clothing for every nation that toured.

The colours themselves became a shorthand. The West Indies moved to a more traditionally masculine maroon. New Zealand settled into a comfortable beige-brown. And Australia, of course, donned the infamous 'canary yellow' variant of Australian gold.

By 1992, World Cups were all-colour affairs. A rainbow of nations doing multi-pigmented battle for cricketing supremacy. Cricket kits became fashion items, debated and discussed and (eventually) purchased on eBay by dedicated fans.

When T20 tournaments began to take root around the world, they came with market-researched colour schemes. In the early years of such competitions, in fact, it was far easier to refer to sides by their colours. 'Red Melbourne' and 'Green Melbourne', 'Pink Sydney' and 'Green Sydney' were easier to remember than 'Stars', 'Thunder', 'Sixers' and 'Renegades'.

Colour kits became entrenched as part of the shorter formats. It even had some fans and commentators asking whether teams needed alternate kits to avoid colour clashes. (Answer: no. The ones with the big lumps of wood in their hands remain part of the batting team. The rest are fielders.)

And it can all be traced back to that first World Series Cricket match in 1979.

The match itself was uninspiring, cricket-wise. But cracking in terms of meaningless adherence to rules. Australia batted first and made 9/149

from their fifty overs. Even that lowly total represented something of a recovery. When Rod Marsh was bowled by Richard Austin, they'd been 7/88.

But Ian Chappell had teamed up with Dennis Lillee to scramble their way to something at least vaguely defensible. Then rain arrived. The rain and the lack of modern understanding about how to most fairly adjust run rates blew any defensibility theory away. When play resumed, the West Indies still needed the same three runs an over they were originally seeking. But now over the much shorter time-frame of 16 overs. And with all ten wickets in hand.

This is precisely the kind of simplified calculation that the Duckworth–Lewis–Stern methodology has stamped out. Had the DLS formula been in play back then, the West Indies would have needed to chase a fairer target of 71 from 16 overs, with ten wickets in hand.

However, these were simpler times. Needing just 48 runs from 16 overs, the West Indies cruised to the target. They took only nine overs to get there. This was despite the best efforts of Len Pascoe, who managed to dismiss Viv Richards, Clive Lloyd and Lawrence Rowe before the target was reached.

Yet even this wasn't the end of it. Because some official got it in their head that if the teams didn't play a minimum of 15 overs each, then the match wouldn't qualify as legitimate. This was rather a daring misinterpretation of the whole 'minimum number of overs needed to constitute a match' playing condition. Usually, if a team is skilful enough to reach their target in a shorter number of overs, one doesn't punish them by declaring the match to be null and void.

But, again, these were simpler times. (And we shouldn't mock our more innocent forebears too much. As recently as 2007, the officials at an actual *World Cup freakin' final* got themselves all muddled up about how to interpret the rules concerning reserve days. This led to the farcical situation of an Australian side lobbing down gentle off-spin in the dark before being given permission to celebrate a trifecta of World Cup victories.)

So, bizarrely, the West Indies were forced to head back out onto the ground. They were asked to bat on, despite already having won the match.

And that wasn't the end of it either. Because local council by-laws meant the lights would be turned off at 10.30 pm. And there was no way Australia could bowl their required 15 overs in the short amount of time remaining.

In fact, they bowled only three more, with the West Indies finishing on 4/65 off 12 overs. At this point, the umpires apparently completely changed their mind on the whole 'both sides need to bowl 15 overs' idea. They awarded the West Indies the victory they should have received three overs earlier. Then they signed off on the historically baffling scorecards and headed home, locking up the stadium and turning off the lights as they did so.

A colourful match indeed.

NEXT:

Limited-overs matches aren't the only formats in which cricket evolves. Test matches can showcase innovation too. Plus, butcher's shop offcuts!

SARFRAZ NAWAZ
TAKES 7/1

Reverse Swing

THE MOMENT:

On the final day of the first Test against Pakistan in 1979, Australia's march to victory is undone by a spell from Sarfraz Nawaz in which he takes 7/1

After the World Series Cricket summer in Australia concluded in 1979, Kerry Packer packed up his circus. He then flew the WSC Australia team over to tour the West Indies. The WSC World XI, meanwhile, was dispersed into its constituent parts. With a sheepish smile on their collective faces, the various international players returned to their national sides.

This was convenient for Pakistan, who were about to begin their tour of Australia. Unlike the Australian officials, the Pakistani selectors had no qualms in picking WSC players. And so Asif Iqbal, Imran Khan, Javed Miandad, Majid Khan, Mushtaq Mohammed and Zaheer Abbas all rejoined the Pakistan national side. They were to face a second-tier Australia side that had spent the summer losing the Ashes 5–1.

The final WSC player to rejoin Pakistan was the tall, right-arm fast-medium bowler Sarfraz Nawaz. Despite being part of the WSC World XI squad, Sarfraz hadn't played in the SuperTests against Australia. Instead, Imran Khan provided the sole Pakistani bowling option in those matches.

Based on the evidence of the first Test against the official Australian side, his absence had been a lucky break for their colourful WSC counterparts.

Sarfraz's impact on the first four days of the Test was solid but inconspicuous. He arrived at the crease in Pakistan's first innings with the visitors in trouble at 7/122. He combined with Imran Khan for a 51-run partnership to take the score to 8/173, before he was the last man out. His solid 35 helped Pakistan to 196.

In reply, Australia were bowled out for 168, with Sarfraz taking the last two wickets to fall. Pakistan then made 9/353, declaring midway through the fourth day. Australia had been set 382 runs for victory.

The run chase began well. Sarfraz took the first two wickets, bowling both openers, but not before 109 runs were on the board. A run-out of captain Graham Yallop early on the fifth day saw Australia dip to 3/128. However, future captains Allan Border and Kim Hughes then combined. The pair took Australia deep into the final session, and to the brink of victory.

When Australia reached 3/305 with an hour and a half remaining, only 77 runs were required for victory. The depleted Australians could nervously contemplate a stirring victory. That's when Sarfraz returned for a new spell.

Taking the old ball, Sarfraz bowled Border off the inside edge for 105, before having injured batter Graeme Wood caught behind first ball.

Then he began swinging it. But swinging it the wrong way. It was the first time anybody had seen reverse swing, and the batters had not a single idea how to deal with it. Peter Sleep was bowled for a duck with a yorker. Hughes tried to hit out, but was caught at mid-off for 84. Wayne Clark then went first ball to another reverse-swinging yorker. Sarfraz had taken five wickets for no run in thirteen balls.

Over the next few overs, he carelessly allowed a run from wicketkeeper Kevin Wright to ruin his figures. But he soon picked up the last pair of tailenders to finish with 7/1 from the spell, and 9/86 overall. Australia were all out for 310, and Pakistan had won the Test by 71 runs.

Reverse swing took a while to catch on. (Sarfraz actually denied that his match-winning spell had used reverse swing at all. But, as the old saying goes, if it curves in late like a duck, yorks batters like a duck and immediately dismisses every tailender that faces it for a duck . . .)

For a time, reverse swing was passed down from Pakistani fast bowler to Pakistani fast bowler. Imran Khan, Wasim Akram and Waqar Younis all wielded it expertly. But eventually reverse swing escaped the knowledge confines of Pakistan. It spread throughout the cricketing world, becoming a fresh weapon in the fast bowler's arsenal.

Historically, it had been spinners who built their career around deception and variations, googlying, flippering and zootering down deliveries with the barest of provocation. Fast bowlers are less reliant on deception. By bowling faster than spinners, they reduce the reaction time available to the batter, and therefore need smaller deviations in path and expectations to have an impact.

But reverse swing provided a new fast bowler's variation, and it's now so prevalent that it's arguably the dominant form of swing bowling. So much so that we should now consider 'reverse swing' the standard form of swing. And that means what is currently regular swing should be recalibrated as the new 'reverse'. If nothing else, it would confuse older fans of the game – always useful to keep them on their toes.

Another trick fast bowlers added to their repertoire was to stop being so darn fast. Slower balls became a go-to variation. Simon O'Donnell and Steve Waugh developed potent back-of-the-hand versions back in the mid-1980s. As with reverse swing, slower balls spread far and wide, becoming a standard tactic in the death overs of a limited-overs match. Different versions evolved. Knuckle balls, palm balls, leg and off cutters, split-fingers. All named for offcuts in the most disgusting bargain tray at the local butcher's shop.

All the slower balls shared the same goal: to make batters look like buffoons as they slogged too early at a delivery that hadn't yet arrived. But sometimes slower balls also went wrong. Bad slower balls tended to result in a slow full toss that the batter could pick early and loft into the crowd for six. Still, any delivery that could easily result in either the batter *or* the bowler coming across as utterly incompetent is bound to be a popular one.

'Bowl it slower, Shoaib!' the fans cry. 'Let's see one out of the back of your hand, Binga!'

The proliferation of slower-ball varieties opened the door for other bowlers to use change-ups. That's when they suddenly bowl faster than expected. A reverse slower ball, if you will.

Ultimately, the lesson from all these variants is that the key to success as a bowler is simple: always bowl the most unexpected delivery you have available to you. Even if — *especially* if — that's what the batter expects you to do.

NEXT:

Bowlers have reverse swing. Batters have reverse sweeps. Plus, wayward safari tourists!

MIKE GATTING

REVERSE SWEEPS ALLAN BORDER

Invented Shots

THE MOMENT:

In the 1987 World Cup final, desperate Australian captain Allan Border brings himself on to bowl, and succeeds first ball when Mike Gatting reverse-sweeps a catch to the keeper

There was a time when reverse sweeps were considered the last refuge of the mentally deranged.

There was also a time when England captain Mike Gatting's most infamous moment at the crease had nothing whatsoever to do with Shane Warne.

Those two times intersected at the 1987 World Cup final. Gatting was on 41 from 44 balls, effortlessly guiding his side past the halfway mark of a run chase against the plucky underdog Australians. Then, for no clear reason, he played a reverse sweep to Allan Border's first ball.

The delivery from the desperate Border was a wayward one, angled well down the leg side. It would have been called a wide had Gatting let it pass. But Gatting couldn't help but pick at it. He somehow smacked the ball into his own shoulder, where it lobbed up for a simple catch. England's chase collapsed and Australia won their first World Cup. They would never be loveable underdogs at such a tournament again.

Reverse sweeps were already frowned upon at that point in cricketing history. But the frowns furrowed ever deeper into English brows with this World Cup–losing point of evidence against them.

In contrast, in modern times, Glenn Maxwell can switch-hit the first ball he faces for a six. Or, equally likely, into the hands of an outfielder. Either way, viewers will smile and shrug and say, 'That's the way he plays.'

The disapproval of reverse sweeps and other improper variants has been chipped away over the decades. This can, of course, be traced back to Darwinian evolution. In particular, the Red Queen effect.

Most people think the Red Queen effect refers to Her Majesty's embarrassment during the 1990s whenever she attended Lord's to watch the England team's mortifying attempts to play cricket.

Not so. In fact, the Red Queen effect is a concept biologists shamelessly stole from the author of *Alice's Adventures in Wonderland*, Lewis Carroll. The thieving scientists use it to describe a phenomenon where two competing organisms must adapt and evolve not to gain any meaningful advantage over each other, but merely to keep pace with each other. Predators must keep getting faster in order to catch prey. Prey must continue to get faster to avoid being eaten by predators. Predators must keep getting faster in order to catch prey. Prey must—

You get the idea. Each generation becomes objectively better at hunting (or avoiding being hunted) than their predecessors. But it does no good.

There's no relative advantage gained by either side of the hunter–hunted equation. Or, if there is an advantage, it's a short-lived one that soon reverts to an equilibrium.

The Red Queen effect exists in cricket, too. Especially in limited-overs matches. Because that's where the known, finite lifespan of an innings fosters the necessary environment for adaptive innovation.

In Test cricket, bowlers are considered the predators and batters their prey. Hence, a bowling 'attack'. Limited-overs matches flip this. The bowlers are now defending a total and batters are looking to attack and take runs from them.

Limited resources drive evolutionary behaviour in the non-cricket world. A lion with a buffet of zebras, wildebeest and wayward safari tourists to choose between has no incentive to become a stronger, faster, wilier hunter. But if there are only a few skittish antelope, ready to scamper at the first scent of a predator, then only the best lions will survive to pass on their genes.

Similarly, in the cricket world, the limited resources of the 300 deliveries in an ODI and the 120 in a T20 force batters to evolve. But batters are not just competing against opposition bowlers. They're also competing with the scoring rates of the opposition

batters. Furthermore, they're also trying to outscore their *own* teammates. This fosters a powerful competitive environment for evolution. Survival of the switch-hittest.

And so the array of batting strokes implemented by batters develops. They premeditatedly swing through the line in the death overs. They Dilscoop balls over their heads to unpatrolled areas of the field. And they reverse-sweep and switch-hit like nobody's business.

While the result is often similar, there *is* a difference between a switch hit and a reverse sweep. That difference boils down to grip. For a reverse sweep, a batter keeps their original grip while playing the shot in the opposite direction to what the fielding team expects. A switch hit accomplishes the same goal by having the batter switching their grip (and their stance). The switch transforms them from right-handed to left-handed (or, where applicable, vice versa).

Switching grips and stances in this fashion has caused some controversy over the years. Ian Chappell, for example, has claimed that every time a batter attempts a switch hit, the delivery should be declared a dead ball. Chappell's argument is that it's unfair that a batter can switch his handedness to make the bowler's field placings redundant.

It's a weird stance to take. One might be tempted to say that it's the reverse of the stance we might expect.

Batters trying to hit the ball where fielders aren't isn't some pox on the game, but rather the goal of all batters since time immemorial. The switch hit is merely the latest evolution of this fundamental batting tactic. Any debate about whether the shot is brilliant or unfair misses the point. A well-executed switch hit is brilliant *and* unfair.

If the authorities want to keep a balance between bat and ball, they shouldn't limit what batters can do in terms of handedness. They should instead expand what *bowlers* can do. Let them bowl with either hand, or change from over the wicket to around the wicket without warning. Make more things possible, not fewer.

The existence of the switch hit doesn't unlock an unbeatable cheat code to the game. If it did, every batter would be switch-hitting every single delivery. But of course a switch hit shot, like any other shot in the game, can be poorly executed.

Which brings us all the way back to poor old Mike Gatting and his reverse sweep.

In his thinking, Gatting may well have been ahead of his time with his shot choice, aiming to hit the ball into a gap where the fielders weren't. But his execution brought him undone. And it cost England a World Cup.

When it comes to infamous moments at the crease while facing spin, most batters would be content with this being their peak. It's to Gatting's eternal credit that he would later scale even greater heights of spinfamy.

NEXT:

Batters can come up with weird shots to play. Or they can just have weird bats with which to play them. Plus, Paul Simon ad campaigns!

DENNIS LILLEE WIELDS AN ALUMINIUM BAT

Bats

THE MOMENT:

In the first Test against England in the 1979/80 summer, Dennis Lillee briefly bats with the ComBat – a cricket bat made of aluminium

For the summer of 1979/80, the Australian Cricket Board and World Series Cricket had made peace. One of the agreements in the peace treaty was that both England and the West Indies would tour Australia for Test series. (Other concessions included: Channel Nine having television rights, a ten-year contract for a new Packer company to market the game, and the older boys getting to make fun of Kim Hughes again.)

Both the West Indies and England would play three-Test series against Australia. However, the home side's opponents would be alternated throughout the summer like the French braids of the most sophisticated girl in school. Those Tests would also be randomly interspersed with a triangular one-day series between the three sides, like the unruly follicles of a far more ostracised schoolgirl.

Furthermore, Australia's Test series against England would not have the Ashes at stake. England had already won them earlier that year. The idea of competing for the Ashes twice in the same year was too old-fashioned to consider (it had last happened in the summers of 1920/21 and 1921). Or possibly too far ahead of its time (the twin Ashes series of 2013 and 2013/14 had yet to be invented). Or maybe too clean-sweep-risky (both the 1920/21 and the 2013/14 Ashes had seen Australia win 5–0.)

With no Ashes at stake, the series ascended into farce early on the second day of the first Test. After three uneventful deliveries from Ian Botham, Lillee drove the fourth ball down the ground for three.

The bat with which he'd played the shot was made of aluminium. It was called the ComBat. Not because it was sponsored by the Commonwealth Bank. But rather because in the 1970s this was considered a neat piece of wordplay on the word 'combat'.

The ComBat was manufactured by a friend of Lillee's, and the fast bowler had agreed to use it in the Test to help promote it. (If it had been developed seven years later, it may have instead been marketed with a sophisticated television advertising campaign set to Paul Simon's toe-tapping single 'You Can Call Me Al'. Assuming, of course, that they wanted to market it to the niche cross-section of cricketers who were fans of periodic table element symbols.)

The shot down the ground drew immediate concerns from both captains. Mike Brearley, the England captain, found the metallic *ding* of bat hitting ball worrisome. He immediately protested to the umpires that the DingBat would damage the ball.

In the dressing rooms, Australian captain Greg Chappell had different concerns. From where he was sitting, he felt Lillee's shot should have gone all the way to the boundary for four. The fact that it didn't suggested the bat had no life in it. He immediately sent twelfth man Rodney Hogg out with a normal everyday wooden bat to replace Lillee's NumBat. Lillee refused until Chappell went down to make the demand in person. Lillee, cool-headed as ever, acceded to his captain's in-person request by hurling the aluminium bat towards the pavilion.

Lillee's heroic attempt to bring *Air Bud* rules to cricket bats had met with failure. Much like there 'ain't no rules says a dog can't play basketball', at the time there also 'ain't no rules says a cricket bat needs to be made of wood'. Shortly after, of course, those exact rules were added. (The cricket wooden bat rules, that is. The rules around hoop-shooting canines remain vague.)

But Lillee's aluminium wasn't the end of equipment evolution. Balls grew whiter, and then pink. They had different stitching on different brands of balls, producing different amounts of swing. Bats, meanwhile, settled for growing bigger. If they were to be limited in material to wood, they were going to be as woody as possible. Modern players like big bats. And

they cannot lie. (Ha ha ha. No, that's not true. Modern players are no Sir or Dame Mix-A-Lots. They can indeed lie. As anybody who has seen the caught behind appeals initiated solely to try to trick umpires out of calling wides could tell you.)

There's a photo that circulated a few years ago of South African legend Barry Richards holding the bat with which he made 325 in a day at the WACA in 1970 alongside David Warner's bat. Warner's is a Schwarzenegger of a thing in comparison to Richards's de Vitoesque willow. The monstrousness of modern cricket bats helps explain why sixes are more prevalent than ever before.

But it only *helps* explain it. It doesn't resolve the whole thing. That's because big bats are not the only reason for the proliferation of sixes. Big bats have also, for example, coincided with unprecedented professionalism of players. Batters have more time and greater incentive for gym work, building muscles that make them more likely to brute-force the ball over the rope.

The rope itself is another reason why there are more sixes, of course. Players don't have to hit the ball quite as far in the modern game to register a six as they did in an era where the ball had to clear an actual fence. But again, this is only a part-reason. Because a sizeable proportion of sixes not only clear the ropes but threaten the crowds.

The final reason has to do with mindset. Players have learned over the years that the balance between risk and runs is more biased towards the latter than they once thought.

It's why a decent ODI innings in the 1980s of something around 230 is considered laughably below par these days. Batters now know that they can score faster without any concomitant increase in risk.

Cricket, as we've mentioned before, tests the minds of players as much as their physical skills. Knowing you are capable of hitting a six and having the courage to attempt the shot are as important as having a big bat with which to hit it. Of course, it's also easier to be courageous when you have a bat with a sweet spot so large and edges so thick that even a mishit can fly over the rope.

If nothing else, you don't have to fear your captain charging onto the field and ordering you to use the more powerful bat being offered to you by Rodney Hogg. That has to count for something, surely.

NEXT:

You have always been able to replace a bat. Until recently, however, it was much harder to replace a batter. Plus, schlock swamp monsters!

MARNUS LABUSCHAGNE REPLACES STEVE SMITH

Substitutions

THE MOMENT:

In the second Test of the 2019 Ashes, England fast bowler Jofra Archer's bouncer strikes Steve Smith, concussing him and opening the door for Marnus Labuschagne to become the first ever concussion substitute

Steve Smith seemed unstoppable. Not even Bradman's record of 974 runs in a Test series felt out of reach.

Actually, Smith *had* been stopped twice already in the series, but only after reaching 140 in both innings of the first Test. It's possible Smith had been spurred on by the tiresome booing and sandpaper-waving from the Barmy Army. Their soldiers were very keen to get in on all the SandpaperGate joking a year and a half after everybody else had already worked the material to death.

Alternatively, Smith may have been oblivious to the Barmy Army's belated taunting. He seemed impervious to their mockery, batting inside a cocoon of eccentric leaves, like some kind of schlock swamp monster.

Either way, all we can know for sure is that their hack material didn't negatively impact his batting.

In the first innings of the first Test, Smith had helped Australia recover from 8/122 to reach 284. In the second he'd provided the backbone of Australia's 7/487 declared. The pair of 140s had been enough for Australia to take the first Test by 251 runs.

In the second Test, England added speedster Jofra Archer to their side to make his Test debut. Archer had already won a World Cup for his nation that summer, bowling the Super Over that had given England the trophy.

His addition for the Test didn't make much difference at first. Again, the rest of Australia collapsed in their first innings. Again, Smith was leading a recovery. He'd reached 80, giving him 366 runs for the series in his three innings, when Archer hit him.

Smith had already been struck on the elbow by an Archer delivery a little earlier. There were initial fears from the dressing room then that he'd broken his arm. The fears when the ball hit Smith's head went to a much darker place. Everybody in world cricket was very aware of the potential consequences of such a blow. Some of the Australian players (David Warner, Nathan Lyon and Travis Head) had played in the 2014 Sheffield Shield match in which Phillip Hughes had sustained the blow to the head that cost him his life.

So there was enormous relief when Smith stood and walked off the ground, retiring hurt to the dressing room. There, he passed the initial concussion protocols. This allowed him to return at the fall of Peter Siddle's wicket and smoke three further boundaries, before being dismissed for 92.

By the next morning, however, Smith's condition had worsened and he failed a concussion test. Under new ICC regulations, Australia were allowed a 'like for like' replacement. The man most like Steve Smith in the squad was deemed to be Marnus Labuschagne. This seemed inexplicable at the time. But, regardless, Labuschagne got to fill the role of the best Test batter in the world for the final day of the Test.

Labuschagne took the 'like for like' role very seriously indeed. To the point of also copping a delivery from Archer flush on the grille when he was finally summoned to the crease at 2/19 in Australia's second innings, late on the fifth day. But his determination to emulate Smith was kept under control. Labuschagne immediately bounced to his feet to pass a concussion test. He went on to score 59 to ensure Australia escaped the Test with a draw.

Smith was ruled out of the third Test. This was a decision backed up by the medical advice of every England fan. Many of these concerned part-time doctors went so far as to further rule him out of the rest of the series. Maybe even the next Ashes in Australia too. Can't be too careful.

Fortunately for Australia, Labuschagne's return to Test cricket saw everything the young batter touch turn to gold. The Marnus Touch.

Labuschagne had averaged a mere 26.25 from five Tests before his concussion substitute role. His post-concussion era saw him soon became Australia's second-most important batter. (And also a handy leg-spinner: he took a key wicket in the dying overs of the fourth Test that ensured Australia retained the Ashes.)

Labuschagne soon became the first batter in 2019 to reach 1000 Test runs (= one kilorun). But M'ing up (as the kids and the Romans like to say) with the bat in 2019 was not all that Labuschagne offered. No, the Marnus Cinematic Universe was filled with as much eccentricity and weirdness as the batting world occupied by Smith.

For example, Labuschagne was soon spotted touching the bails whenever he first came to the crease. His explanation was that it was because Chadd Sayers had bowled him with balls that had clipped the stumps. As a result, Labuschagne could no longer abide bails hanging outside the off-stump line. Instead, he'd make sure each one was tucked in tight with the stump.

Lots of players work on 'the one-percenters', things that make a tiny difference to their game. Labuschagne was working on the 0.01 percenters. But as weird as it all seemed – and it got weirder, with shouts of 'no run' after leaves, and reports of wanting to take toasted sandwiches onto the field in his pocket – it worked.

Labuschagne soared up the batting averages and rankings. Almost to the point where it seemed possible that people might stop referring to Smith as 'the best since Bradman' and start referring to him as 'the best between Bradman and Marnus'.

Despite his rise, Labuschagne's biggest impact still came from his concussion substitution. And not in the obvious ways. Because Labuschagne was not only the first concussion substitute. It had become clear that he was also the most like-for-likiest substitute imaginable.

So much so that he set a near-impossible standard for future concussion substitutes to live up to. In a T20I in Australia the following summer, India brought Yuzvendra Chahal in as a concussion substitute for Ravindra Jadeja. Chahal subsequently conjured up a

player-of-the-match performance. Australian fans immediately conjured up cries of foul.

And it wasn't just Australian fans. The Australian coach, Justin Langer, got into the debate too. He was spotted remonstrating with match referee David Boon about the replacement.

(This was actually a beautiful full circle moment for the pair. In Langer's first Test, Boon advised him – Langer – to retire hurt after he – Langer – was struck on the head first ball. He – still Langer – refused. Thirty years of concussion debates and the two were still at loggerheads.)

Despite the complaints, it was difficult to see what, exactly, the issue was with the Chahal replacement. India had ten minutes between the change of innings to assess Jadeja's concussion and find a substitute.

Under those constraints, they chose the player who was (a) close enough in style (bowls spin) and (b) gave the team the best chance of winning. Most importantly, Chahal was a substitute who (c) the match referee agreed was okay.

Cricket has been evolving ever since its birth. As we've seen, most of that evolution is driven by money and its conjoined sibling, television ratings. When there's an innovation such as concussion substitutes that is driven instead by concerns for the wellbeing of players, that should be encouraged. Not shut down by pedantic squabbling over degrees of similarity between players.

Expecting every other nation to subscribe to a like-for-like standard at the Marnus-for-Smith level is too much. Getting in the right general vicinity of like-for-like should be enough. After all, not every country has substitute players going full *Single White Female* on their injured star batter.

NEXT:

Rule changes and player experimentation force cricket to evolve. They also drive captains to explore new tactics. Plus, pandemic toilet paper!

THE TACTICS OF CRICKET

MONTY PANESAR

PANESAR

CHANGES
HIS GLOVES

Time Wasting

THE MOMENT:

In the first Test of the 2009 Ashes, James
Anderson and Monty Panesar waste
enough time in the final hour of the match
to secure a miraculous draw

Australia showed up in England for the 2009 Ashes confident of victory. Oh, sure. The last time they'd toured, in 2005, they'd lost possession of the urn in one of the most electrifying series in the history of Test cricket.

But their response to that shock defeat had been brutal: a 5–0 clean sweep of the 2006/07 Ashes back in Australia. Their assorted superstars, Ponting, Gilchrist, Warne and McGrath, had taken it in turns to show those impudent Englishmen who was boss.

Warne and McGrath had retired at the end of that redemption arc (yes, yes, and Justin Langer too). Gilchrist departed the summer after. But Ponting still led a talented squad to English shores in 2009. Despite the odd series defeat to India and South Africa, Australia were the number-one side in the ICC rankings, and expected to dominate.

And dominate they did! Eight centuries to England's two, reflecting the fact that Australian batters occupied six of the top seven run-scoring slots for the series. On the bowling front, Australia also had the top three wicket-takers for the series. Furthermore, wicketkeeper Brad Haddin secured three more dismissals than his English counterpart, Matt Prior, despite playing one fewer Test.

This ascendancy was reflected in the average runs and wickets over the course of the series. Australia scored their runs at an average of 40.65 per wicket, significantly superior to England's average of 34.15.

It was a dominant performance by the Australian side. They must therefore have been somewhat startled to discover at the end of the series that they would be returning home without the Ashes. Again. Because, somehow, despite the statistical dominance of Ponting's men, England won the series 2–1, with two Tests drawn.

Of those two drawn Tests, it was the first, the series opener, that hurt most.

England won the toss and batted, reaching a respectable 435 in their first innings. Australia responded with an enormous 6/674, declaring shortly before tea on the fourth day. Ponting made 150, with Simon Katich, Brad Haddin and an unbeaten Marcus North also adding centuries to the tally.

England, 239 behind on the first innings, were 2/20 by tea, when rain stopped play. Then 5/102 at lunch on the final day. But Paul Collingwood combined with the lower order to send the match into the last hour. However, he fell with eleven overs remaining in the match, caught by a juggling

Mike Hussey. It left England with one wicket remaining, still six runs behind.

It took the tailenders 25 balls to wipe off those six runs. James Anderson eventually squirted Peter Siddle through the slips cordon for consecutive boundaries. This changed the equation of the match. With England ahead, Australia would have to bat again to win the Test. That would subtract ten minutes from the match for the innings break. Australia had bowled their overs in the final hour quickly. But the lost ten minutes meant if England could survive to 6.41 pm, the match would be drawn.

This opened the door for mischief. Suddenly, gloves needed to be changed at every opportunity. Physios needed to be consulted on freshly discovered ailments. Post-match dinner reservations needed to be booked.

Time, in short, needed to be wasted.

The amount of time in which cricket isn't played is one of the ongoing issues that fans of the sport grapple with. In limited-overs matches, there's little to gain from time-wasting, unless rain is imminent. The match is defined by the number of overs to be bowled.

But Test cricket is limited by time. When time runs out, if there's no result, the match is drawn. And if you're about to lose a Test, the oasis of a draw is enticing indeed, beckoning a desperate team down the path of wasting time.

Technically, time-wasting is against the Laws of Cricket, but it's proven impossible to police over the years. It's also technically against the Spirit of Cricket too. You can't get more evasive of the basic bat and ball confrontation of cricket than not actually playing. But time-wasting is not as decried as other spiritual violations because it's a tool that's available to both sides.

Sometimes, as at Cardiff in 2009, it's the batters who want to slow things down. At other times it's in the fielding side's interest to minimise the amount of actual play.

And both sides can accomplish their time-wasting goals more or less effortlessly. Batters can have mid-pitch chats, or can call for a new helmet or bat or gloves, or do some farming of the pitch, or go down with cramp, or move the sightscreen, or simply pull away as the bowler runs in. Bowlers, meanwhile, can change their fields, complain about the shape of the ball, abort their run-ups, change their fields, ask for the landing area on the crease to be bolstered with sawdust, and then change their field some more.

There are, it seems, more ways to not play cricket than there are to play it. So when the match situation demands it, the best cricket players will play as little cricket as possible.

The versatility of time-wasting as a tactic is why umpires, match referees and administrators struggle to find ways to stamp it out. Whatever fines or penalties they threaten to impose for slow over rates are far too often suspended. A case can always be made that it's never the fielding team's fault.

Players might fume when their opponents do it, as Ponting did in Cardiff. But deep in their heart, they know they'd do the same thing in an instant. It's the cricketing equivalent of stocking up on toilet paper at the beginning of a global pandemic. Maddening when others do it, but a tactic you want to keep up your sleeve in case you ever need it yourself. (Note: do *not* store toilet paper in your sleeves.)

So the time-wasting stalemate holds. It's integrated into the game, another tactical element to take into consideration as part of the contest.

Australia might have had the superior cricket side in 2009, as reflected by their dominance in the statistics. But ultimately, England regained the Ashes because they had a team superior at *not* playing cricket when it counted.

NEXT:

Players can waste time if they put their minds to it. But sometimes time is lost for reasons outside the players' control. Plus, mathematical sanity wands!

BRIAN MCMILLAN

NEEDS 22 RUNS OFF ONE BALL

Rain

THE MOMENT:

In the semi-final of the 1992 World Cup between England and South Africa at the SCG, pre-Duckworth-Lewis rain rules convert South Africa's target from 22 off 13 balls to 22 off 1 ball

'Rain is grace; rain is the sky descending to the earth; without rain, there would be no life,' said American novelist, poet and founding Barmy Army member John Updike.

Cricket journalist and canonised saint Basil of Caesarea similarly pointed out: 'Many a man curses the rain that falls upon his head, and knows not that it brings abundance to drive away the hunger.'

And, of course, ex-Spice Girl and ECB fitness coordinator Geri Halliwell exuberantly exclaimed: 'It's raining, men! Hallelujah!'

But this trio of pluviophiles aren't alone. At some point, cricket makes rain-lovers of us all.

At first glance, this seems implausible. After all, cricket is one of those rare sports that abandons play as soon as precipitation rears its damp, mussed-up head. An absence of cricket being played would, on the surface, appear to be a negative for a fan of the game.

But in fact those delays caused by rain add yet another captivating element to the sport. This isn't lunch, tea, drinks, a change of innings or a CEAT Tyres Strategic Timeout. No, a rain delay is bigger than any scheduled or match-enforced break. Because the weather is fickle and out of our control. It's a meteorological dice roll that can transform the match, opening up exciting new tactical options. Tactical options which can, conveniently, be contemplated while sitting around waiting for the rain to stop.

Cricket has always had rain-based tactics. In the Ancient Times, pitches were uncovered. The arrival of rain could transform an otherwise normal batting pitch into an unplayable quagmire. This, in turn, would transform the Test into a battle of declarations. Canny captains strove to have ball in hand until the sticky wicket became hard again. (This is not as rude a sentence as it sounds.)

The arrival of rain could reverse a team's fortunes. Or, at the very least, one's batting order. That was the tactic Donald Bradman employed in the 1937/38 Ashes against one particular sticky wicket. The tactic meant that the tailenders bore the worst of the pitch. It also allowed The Don to come in at seven and stake a claim on yet another batch of individual batting records. Because he was an insatiable glutton for such things.

But that same era also finally saw the demise of the timeless Test. From that point on, Tests would always contain time. Which meant that time could always be removed from a Test.

And this is Test cricket as we know it today. Where a draw is always an option and, hence, rain can always transform the game. (Or, if you're Hansie Cronje, open up sweet leather jacket–acquiring opportunities.)

There are very few Tests where a perfectly timed burst of rain wouldn't make the match more strategically interesting. Rain gives the stronger team an extra challenge to manoeuvre around, and the weaker team a potential escape route.

Every Test cricket fan has at some point wished for rain to come and save their side. And when such a prayer is answered, there is a disproportionate degree of satisfaction in the outcome. An outplayed team salvaging a draw thanks to a *deus ex precipita* seems almost to be blessed by the Fates themselves. And, deep down, we all know it's better to be lucky than to be competent at cricket.

So far, this only applies to rain delays in Test cricket. This is because, as any elite cricketer will tell you, Test rain delays are the ultimate form of rain delays. Limited-overs rain delays, be they ODI or T20, are dull matters these days. And we have three men to blame for this: Frank Duckworth, Tony Lewis and professor-come-lately Steven Stern.

In a way, the Duckworth–Lewis–Stern method is almost *too* fair a system. There may be some quibbles over the exact size of any given DLS target. Overall, however, there's little doubt that it takes the match state prior to the rain and accurately reflects that state in the post-downpour revised target.

As such, all we're left with is a time jump, with no new tactical elements added to the game. Sure, maybe while it's been raining we've been shown some highlights from an old match. Or watched a (flawed) Classic Catches segment. Or listened to commentators fill time while waiting for the next radar update by selecting ludicrous squads for whatever ICC tournament looms next. So it's not time wasted. But nothing fundamental about the game has been altered.

It wasn't always this way, of course. Before Duckworth and Lewis waved their mathematical sanity wands over the playing conditions, rain delays could cause all kinds of mad and unfair outcomes.

The best known, of course, is the 22 runs off 1 ball target adjustment from the 1992 World Cup semi-final between South Africa and England. (In fact, the adjusted target should have been 21 off 1 ball. The SCG scoreboard had it wrong.) This was blatantly silly, but not quite as unfair as it's generally painted to be.

South Africa weren't naive innocents scuppered by the Most Productive Overs rain rule in vogue at the time. They were, as ever, hard-nosed competitors, willing to push the limits of the Laws and the Spirit of Cricket as far as they could.

They won the toss and elected to field first. Captain Kepler Wessels knew that rain was forecast but was willing to take his chances. By bowling first, he was able to slow down the England innings using all the usual time-wasting techniques.

South Africa's lethargic over rate meant that England's first innings – scheduled to go for the standard 50 overs – was curtailed at 45. The five lost overs denied England the full opportunity to accelerate at the back end of their innings. Off the 45th over, Dermot Reeve added 18 runs to take England to 6/252. It's not inconceivable that they might have broken 300 had South Africa not been so tardy in the field.

South Africa's gamesmanship meant they were chasing 253 for victory off 45 overs. They got to 6/231 with 13 balls remaining when the rain came and cost them the match. The unfairness of the situation was part of what inspired Duckworth

and Lewis to come up with their system in the first place.

The good news for South Africa was that, with two overs lost, the Duckworth–Lewis method would have seen their required target reduced by 16 runs (rather than 0 or 1, depending on whether you trust scorers or SCG big screens).

The bad news? Under Duckworth–Lewis, the five overs that South Africa couldn't be bothered bowling in the first innings would *also* have resulted in a score adjustment. Instead of chasing 252 from 45 overs, South Africa would have been instead in pursuit of a winning target of 273.

In that scenario, their final target would have been 26 off 1 ball. Still impossible, but much more fairly so.

NEXT:

22 (or 26) off 1 ball might seem impossible. But so did beating Steve Waugh's side after following on, and that didn't stop VVS Laxman. Plus, pub trivia cheating!

STEVE WAUGH
ASKS INDIA
TO BAT AGAIN

Follow-ons

THE MOMENT:

In the second Test of the 2001 series against India, Australian captain Steve Waugh enforces the follow-on

Early on the third day of the second Test against India in 2001, Australian skipper Steve Waugh had a fresh decision to make.

He'd captained Australia on twenty-two occasions prior to this Test since taking the mantle two years earlier. Waugh had struggled to define his own leadership style early on. This led to a sluggish start as skipper (two wins, two draws, three losses and one horrific collision with Jason Gillespie in his first seven Tests).

The leadership style upon which he settled was the mightily effective one of gathering together some of the greatest players in Test history. Shane Warne and Glenn McGrath had already established themselves as elite bowlers during the Mark Taylor years. Waugh himself had provided the backbone of much of Taylor's success. But this was insufficient greatness for Waugh's purposes.

And so Adam Gilchrist was summoned forth by Australian Cricket Board druids to singlehandedly transform the role of wicketkeeper. Waugh's eventual successor, Ricky Ponting, returned to the side to begin the most prolific run of a career steeped in prolificity. And Pura Milk Cup (nee Sheffield Shield) sensation Matthew Hayden was added at the top of the order, where he proved he could be just as effective at international, non-dairy-sponsored level.

Waugh's bold strategy of filling a side with some of the most extraordinary cricketers in history bore fruit. His captaincy record turned swiftly positive as Australia completed a record stretch of sixteen successive Test victories.

Yet despite Australia's dominance over that stretch, Waugh had never had the opportunity to enforce the follow-on.

Until the second Test against India in 2001. In reply to Australia's first-innings score of 445, India were bowled out for 171.

(The formula for calculating follow-on targets in a Test match is a simple 200-run deficit. If this seems far too straightforward for a sport that usually revels in needless complexity, fret not. Additional random confusion is added to perplex newcomers by noting that the deficit can be reduced to 150 runs. But only if the first day of the match is washed out.)

Waugh didn't hesitate. Why would he? It had taken his side fewer than 60 overs to bowl out India in the first innings. His attack was fresh and the India batters had shown in the first three innings of the series that they had no answer to them.

Then suddenly, like a smartphone smuggled into a pub trivia

competition, the answers came with game-breaking ease. VVS Laxman, who had top-scored in the first innings with 59, was promoted from number six to first drop. Rahul Dravid had made the next-highest score (25) in the first innings. He switched places with Laxman, coming in at the fall of the fourth wicket.

India were still 42 runs behind Australia's first-innings total when Dravid joined Laxman. By the time the pair were separated, after a full day of batting, India were 334 runs ahead. Laxman finished with 281, Dravid 180.

Australia were cooked. They failed to hold on for the draw on the final day. Then, in the third Test, a resurgent India scraped home to complete a stunning come-from-behind series victory.

As every student of Australian cricket history knows, Waugh learnt his lesson from the Kolkata defeat. He never enforced the follow-on again.

Hmm? What's that? Huh. I'm hearing that, in fact, Waugh enforced the follow-on *seven* further times in his captaincy career. In fact, every single time he had the opportunity to do so. Also, that he won every one of those Tests.

Waugh might have pigheadedly continued to use the follow-on to incorrectly win Tests going forward. But future Australian (and non-Australian) captains were more circumspect.

The Dravid–Laxman klaxon sounded loud and clear.

The India win had highlighted the pros and cons of enforcing follow-ons.

The original reason for the follow-on, and the original risk in not enforcing it, was the prospect of running out of time. In eras when scoring rates were slower, taking time out of the game by batting a second time could open the door for the poorer team to escape with a draw.

The other risk was that the captain might miscalculate the target they set. Nobody wanted to squander the position of dominance that led to the follow-on option with a too-generous declaration. But to feel safe, captains needed to set gigantic fourth-innings targets. Whereas if they enforced the follow-on, those excessive runs would almost always be unnecessary. (Although, of course, still helpful in padding out one's stats against a down-trodden opponent.)

There is also the risk that in not enforcing the follow-on, a muddle-headed captain might simply forget to declare their second innings. Admittedly, an unlikely risk.

But Waugh's side had more or less eliminated all those risks. One of the first acts of his captaincy had been to urge his batters to strive for scoring a minimum of 300 runs in a day. The impact of this was to accelerate the game and pare down the prospects of a draw. The faster rate also meant that there was plenty of time when batting a second time to set an unchaseable fourth-innings target.

Yet, as discussed, even though Waugh had minimised the risks of not enforcing the follow-on, he continued to do so anyway. The old fool. Future captains, however, began to look at the risks of *enforcing* follow-ons. For the most part, they decided they weren't worth it.

The primary risk of enforcing the follow-on is that your bowlers have to take twenty wickets in a row, bowling in two consecutive innings. Back when there were rest days and fewer Tests scheduled back to back, this was a much smaller risk. In the modern era, tiring out your bowlers looms large in the minds of captains.

And so the follow-on, felt to be so full of folly, fell fallow.

It was a victim not of Laxman and Dravid's rare heroics, as most fans think. Rather, it succumbed to the practical realities of negotiating a modern packed Test match schedule.

A shame. Because follow-ons still have a lot to offer. Follow-ons make the game more interesting. They mix up the usual batting order of the sides. More importantly, they offer the prospect of batters being dismissed twice in a day. (Or twice in a session, as happened to Farokh Engineer, during the 1971/72 series between Australia and a Rest of the World team.)

Maybe follow-ons will become fashionable again someday. All it will take is a charismatic international skipper (looking at you, Patrick James Cummins) to lead the way.

Alternatively, if the team in the lead doesn't want to use follow-ons anymore, why not let the team batting second decide if they follow on? That might open up new tactics for captains who are behind in the game.

After all, who better to decide if following on is appropriate than the team that's not leading?

NEXT:

Changing the order of innings in a Test has fallen out of fashion, tactically. Changing the batting order, not so much. Plus, zombified dragons!

JASON GILLESPIE
SCORES A
DOUBLE-CENTURY

Nightwatchmen

THE MOMENT:

In the second Test of the 2006 series against Bangladesh, Jason Gillespie scores 201 not out, the highest ever score by a nightwatchman

A lot of people struggle to understand the logic behind the use of nightwatchmen.

Not surprising. For, according to HBO series *Game of Thrones*, The Night's Watch was a military order, charged with guarding The Wall. This gigantic barricade kept the Seven Kingdoms safe from wildlings and the dreaded White Walkers. And yet the one time they were called upon to do their duty, the fool Nightwatchmen *teamed up* with wildlings. Then succumbed to a zombie ice dragon that breached their defences. This unleashed both the Night King's undead horde and the show's disappointing eighth season on an unsuspecting public.

But as illogical as George RR Martin's nightwatchmen were, cricket's nightwatchmen are even more baffling to many fans.

To nightwatchmen decriers, sending in a less-skilled lower-order batter late in the day makes no sense. How can they 'protect' the batter who would otherwise be due to come to the crease? Surely a better batter is more likely to survive the final overs of a day's play than one with less talent?

And obviously this is true.

For those in favour of their use, the ideal nightwatchman is a lower-order player who can come in late in the evening and survive until stumps. But also not get bogged down the next morning. Once they've seen off the gloom of the night before, they should revert instead to free-scoring batting. And do so until they are dismissed for more or less the score they would have made if they'd come in at their usual place.

This ideal nightwatchman is then a lower-order batter who has a solid defence, but also the ability to score freely when needed. Which is starting to inch them perilously close to being a regular top-order batter. In which case, according to the anti-nightwatchman folk, why not use the scheduled next batter? Y'know, the one who is still more likely to survive the evening in the first place?

The answer is that likeliness of survival isn't the only factor that using a nightwatchman takes into consideration. Yes, a nightwatchman is definitely less likely to survive until stumps. But the impact of losing their wicket is less important than that of losing the wicket of a top-order batter.

That's the benefit of using a nightwatchman. If somebody has to be thrown to the (dire) wolves of fading light, let it be somebody whose runs the team isn't relying upon.

(Again, the exception is Steve Waugh's absurd champion side, who abandoned the practice of using night-watchmen. Waugh's logic was that they had loads of world-class batters in their top seven. Losing one late in the day didn't matter. Plenty more where they came from.)

There are other benefits to using nightwatchmen, at least from a fan's perspective. There's the delicious tactical quandary that takes place if the nightwatchman is dismissed. Should the side send in another one? Or revert to the usual batting order? Or, even more tactically precarious, what if the surviving top-order batter is dismissed? Do you send in a *second* nightwatchman?

The original arguments for using nightwatchmen still hold in these situations. But they now need to be balanced against the diminishing returns of how many lower-order batters in the team actually have the skills to nightwatch. Lots of strategic meat to chew on there.

As much fun as the tactics of using nightwatchmen is to contemplate, that's not the best bit. Because, from a cricket lover's perspective, there's also the prospect of a tailender surviving the evening and then batting on throughout the next day. And, if you're Jason Gillespie, making a double-century.

Gillespie's 201 not out as a night-watchman came against Bangladesh

in 2006. It was a top score more than ten times his batting average, achieved on his thirty-first birthday. (Take *that*, Peter Siddle!)

Bangladesh were bowled out for 197 on the first day (with Gillespie taking 3/11 from his five overs). When Matthew Hayden fell just before stumps, the fast bowler was summoned to the crease to protect captain Ricky Ponting. Gillespie survived the night and then a rain-reduced second day.

On the third day, he brought up his maiden Test century, finishing on 102 not out. Gillespie then batted on into the *fourth* day, where he reached his double-century after lunch. At this point, a merciful Ponting finally declared, with a match-winning 384-run lead.

The best thing about Gillespie's double-century was not only that, in making it, he managed to achieve a higher Test score than that achieved by many of his more illustrious teammates, including Steve Waugh, Mark Waugh, Damien Martyn, Darren Lehmann, David Boon, Mike Hussey et al. It was that Gillespie *knew* he was beating them, and checked them all off with his batting partner, Hussey, as he did so. That's quality double-century-making.

Stranger still, Gillespie never played another Test after this one. Instead, he went on to become a respected, grey-bearded coach instead. (Looking for all the world like a second-tier contender for the Westeros Throne. Some kind of long-lost Baratheon sibling, perhaps?) One can only imagine that he figured he had nothing else to prove as a player.

But nightwatchmen scoring runs is not the best bit about nightwatchmanning, either. No, the most fascinating aspect of nightwatchmannery is how it reverses the usual notion of farming the strike.

Usually when there are two batters at the crease of vastly differing ability, the one with the greater skill tries to take the bulk of the strike. This, in itself, can lead to a captivating tactical subgame. The simple cricketing idea that overs are bowled from alternating ends means that the better batter can't stay on strike the entire time, either smacking boundaries or refusing runs to protect their lesser-skilled partner.

Instead, at the end of each over, they need to manufacture an odd number of runs to retain the strike. And so the straightforward innovation of swapping ends generates compelling cat-and-mouse games of both field and shot placement. That'd be enough for an engrossing sport in and of itself. Instead, it's a tossed-away afterthought for cricket.

But when a nightwatchman is in, this entire subgame flips. An ideal nightwatchman is there not only to protect the next batter due in. Once they're out there, they might as well protect their partner too. After all, exactly the same logic applies.

Which means we now have the lesser batter trying to farm the strike to protect their more skilled teammate. And this complete inversion of the usual process is, somehow, perfectly logically justified.

Stunning to think that simply changing the batting order of a side in response to a day's play coming to an end can have so many intriguing elements to it.

Who watches the nightwatchmen? Everybody who loves cricket, that's who.

NEXT:

Cricket has so many tactical possibilities that you don't even need to be playing the game to use them. Plus, scholastically gifted nerds!

KIM HUGHES

RESIGNS AS CAPTAIN

Press Conferences

THE MOMENT:

After his fifth consecutive defeat to the West Indies, including the first two Tests of the 1984/85 series, an emotional Kim Hughes tenders his resignation from the Australian captaincy

For most of the 20th century, there was a clear hierarchy between film and television. Film was more esteemed, the ultimate goal for any serious actor, director or best boy. Television, in contrast, was schlock for the masses. It was budget entertainment churned out to fill gaps between commercials for McDonald's, Toyota RAV4s and Vicks VapoRub.

Then, around the turn of century, that hierarchy began to shift. The advent of DVD box sets and the ability to watch TV shows at the viewer's discretion (rather than locked in to a specific day and time) invested fans more deeply in shows. The bingeing of their favourites soon justified greater serialisation in television. This, in turn, led to the rise of prestige shows. The length of a season of television had before been a burden that necessitated a formulaic approach to constructing episodes. Now it became a strength, enabling fuller, richer storytelling than the traditional two-hour movie. Instead of glimpses of characters, television now enabled us to get to know them in depth. We could follow their various rises and falls, savouring every moment of the journey.

All of which any Test cricket fan could have told you about *decades* ago.

Because one of the very best things about Test cricket has always been how long it takes. More cricket is obviously better than less cricket (which is why the proper ranking of the various formats is still, and always will be, Test > ODI > T20). But the length of a Test match (let alone a Test series) allows for the development of entire narratives. Storylines as gripping as any season of *The Sopranos*.

One of the side-effects of Test matches and series being played over multiple days is that there are breaks between those days. And, hence, press conferences during those breaks. (In modern times, there are also media interviews during drinks breaks, conducted by flying robots. But let us not get distracted by the magnificent future in which we live.)

For each of those press conferences, the captain is expected to front up and answer questions from the assorted media. This is true regardless of what's happened during the day's play. It doesn't matter if the match is going down to the wire. Or if the team have bowled like madmen. Or if a key wicket has just been lost. Or if the side has collapsed like a house of cards. The press conference must be fronted.

Generally, these press conferences are humdrum affairs. They're bland skippers providing bland sporting clichés for bland match reports. But every now and then a press conference becomes a memorable moment in itself. This is almost always because things are breaking very, very bad.

These are the press conferences where captains resign in tears (Kim Hughes, 1984). Or try to explain why a player has been found with sandpaper in their underpants (Steve Smith, 2018). Or threaten to quit if the team doesn't start improving soon (Allan Border, 1985–1988).

Luckily, such dramatic press conferences are few and far between.

It does, however, open the door for better use of all the other, duller press conferences. Captains should be thinking of these run-of-the-mill press conferences not as a tedious chore to get through at the end of the day's play. No, they should instead approach them as the last opportunity in the day to make an impact on the match. The official companion podcast to the prestige television show.

Cricket is at least 90 per cent a mental game (according to 60 per cent of psychologically trained statisticians and 85 per cent of statistically trained psychologists). The amount of game played in the mind is, as we've mentioned, the entire justification for sledging. If we can get a batter to lose concentration by hurling abuse at them, the argument goes, then they're more likely to make a crucial

misjudgement that leads to them losing their wicket.

But sledging is fraught with peril. It requires a quick wit (or, alternatively, a willingness to unleash a startling variety of cuss words). It needs a keen eye to spot the key moment when sledging might have an impact on the opponent's frame of mind. It has to be targeted enough to upset that frame of mind. But not so boorish that it bounces back on the sledger in the court of public opinion when it's caught by a stump microphone. Oh, and you also have to make sure that you don't drop a catch or get belted for six or make any other kind of error that immediately undoes the impact of the sledge.

In a press conference at the end of a day's play, however, an oratorically adroit captain with skilled scriptwriters can make a proper dent in the opposition's self-confidence. Attacking just outside of stumps. Unleashing a barrage of short quips. Pitching queries up, looking for an edge.

Why settle for an ephemeral on-field sledge that's, in all likelihood, poorly constructed in its phrasing? One whose impact is liable to be lost in the hubbub of the next delivery? It's a wasted use of an international cricketer's brainpower. Especially compared to the more practical option of targeted post-stumps attacks on the opponents' psyches.

Trained writers could spend the day's play writing the press conference monologue. They could use a full repertoire of metaphors, rhetorical questions and other literary techniques designed to linger in minds. Toss in a few high-quality jokes whipped up by seasoned comedy writers to win over the general public. Now you've got a mental attack that can leave a batter second-guessing themselves through-out a sleepless night. *That's* how you win the mental game of cricket.

The support staff for international cricket teams have, in recent years, been extended to include team stat-isticians. These mathematically gifted dorks comb through the data in des-perate search of an edge. It's a small step from there to buttressing the side with the kind of swots who topped the English classes too. Let's give our cricketing jocks a well-rounded group of scholastically accomplished nerds to help them win.

Forget boring old leg-spin and off-spin. The future of cricket is in media spin.

NEXT:

A different kind of tactic outside the hours of play: the overnight declaration. Plus, Foghorn Leghorn!

ALLAN BORDER MAKES A SECOND DECLARATION

Declarations

THE MOMENT:

With a lead of 347 in the second innings, Allan Border declares for the second time in the first Test against India in 1986, leading to the second ever tied Test

A declaration is where a captain wields their most fearsome power. 'No more runs!' they can roar at any moment, embracing their inner monstrous tyrant. With a casual wave of their omnipotent hand, they can end any of their teammates' dreams of individual glory, pitilessly curtailing attempts at breaking records that have stood for generations.

They can also, if they so choose, halt an opponent's stab at a landmark. If a bowler is on a hat-trick or the brink of a five-wicket haul, a well-timed declaration can circumvent their efforts. This option is used more rarely than one might hope – presumably another one of those Spirit of Cricket considerations. A shame, because some days there's no way you can stop a Jim Laker or Anil Kumble from taking all ten wickets. No way, that is, other than by declaring and trapping them forever among the masses of nine-fer commoners.

Another fun thing not enough captains do is close their innings by saying, 'Well, I do declare,' in the drawl of a southern gentleman such as Colonel Sanders or Foghorn Leghorn. To encourage more of this, the ICC should award bonus runs for such mimicry. Especially if a skipper dresses like either of those Confederate heroes while doing so.

Still, declarations aren't all about petty vendettas, churlish denial and dressing as a giant rooster, as fun as those might be. They also have a tactical role in the game. In any given Test match, there are three common opportunities for a declaration. Each has its own delights.

First, there's the first-innings declaration. In most cases, this is pure obnoxious posturing. 'Your bowling attack is insipid and weak,' this declaration declares to the hapless opposition. 'So much so that we can't even be bothered waiting for you to take all our wickets. You could be here forever with your pathetic popgun attack and, frankly, we've got better things to do.'

There's very little risk associated with a first-innings declaration. This makes it the least interesting kind of innings closure. A team can, of course, still lose after declaring on the first innings. Almost always such a defeat will be hilarious (or 'Adelaideriffic', as we call it around these parts). But rarely will the first-innings declaration be looked back upon as the key moment that led to the loss.

So let's move on to the second opportunity for a declaration, conveniently taking place in the second innings. This is where things begin to get a little more intriguing. By now, with both teams having batted, it's possible to get an idea of the quality of the pitch. (Although never as clear an idea as the professionals would have you believe. In almost any given match, the commentators' opinion on what might be a 'par score' is gymnastically flexible.)

There are only two interesting cases for a second-innings declaration. One of those is interesting by virtue of how very dull it is. That's the case where the team batting second has dwarfed the score of the team who batted first. The captain of the second team will therefore aim to declare when they believe they have a sufficient lead to avoid having to bat again, while still retaining enough time to bowl their opponents out. It's got all the same qualities as a third-innings declaration but lacks the erotic frisson of perhaps losing the match. Without that associated risk, this declaration lacks any kind of genuine thrill. It's like trapeze artists using a net or bushwalkers choosing to leave a tiger snake alone. Pointless and tedious.

On the other hand, some captains etch their name into history by declaring behind on the second innings. This is the most dazzling declaration type of them all. The best thing about declaring from behind is that it's secretly not that much riskier than declaring a zillion runs ahead. A declaration from behind is usually made when a pitch is easy to bat on. Most often, the match has already reached the fourth or fifth day without twenty wickets having been taken. It makes the declaring captain look tactically daring, while putting pressure on their counterpart to match their derring-do. 'I dare you to set us a target on this pitch full of runs,' the behind-declaring captain says. 'In fact, I double-dog-dare you.'

Onto the third-innings declaration, then, the best of them all. A third-innings declaration requires the captain to balance all possible outcomes. They need enough time to bowl the opposition out to win, but also enough runs to ensure they don't lose. However, the only way to get more of those loss-denying runs is by taking away some of the win-permitting time. Oh, and furthermore, the quicker your batters can score runs to adjust that balance, the easier the pitch is to bat on. Which means you actually need more runs than you first estimated.

It's an optimisation challenge worthy of humanity's highest-level supercomputers, like Deep Blue, the HAL 9000 or RoboCop. And instead we give it to human cricket captains, most of whom can't even judge when to send the most obvious of DRS reviews upstairs.

Which brings us to Allan Border in 1986. Border had arrived in India straight from a lost series against New Zealand. The Australians' prospects of beating India in India seemed slim indeed.

And yet in the first innings, Australia reached 574 for the loss of seven wickets. Border scored a century, as did David Boon. But most enduringly, a dangerously dehydrated Dean Jones double-tonned up.

Allan Border declared for the first time in the Test at that score, early on the third day. India replied with 397 and Australia batted again, reaching 5/170 at the end of the fourth day.

Overnight, Border declared again. He'd already had the thrill of the first innings 'FFS, if we have to wait for you lot to bowl us out, we could be here all Test' power declaration. Now came the more challenging third-innings declaration. The delicate balance between runs remaining and time remaining in order to take ten wickets.

And Border nailed it. As far as precision declaration calculations go, nobody has ever got it quite as exact as Allan Border on that penultimate night of the Test. He used up all but one ball to take his ten wickets. And every single run.

No captain before him had ever declared with more precision. And no captain has surpassed it since. Border had found the optimal declaration calculation, and the Test would forever be remembered because of it.

Well, that, and the tie thing.

NEXT:

Another tie! Also, why none of these fun tactics actually matters. Plus, frustrated statisticians!

RICHIE BENAUD
GOES FOR THE WIN

Captaincy

THE MOMENT:

With two balls remaining, one run needed to win and one wicket in hand, Joe Solomon runs out Ian Meckiff to tie a Test match for the first time

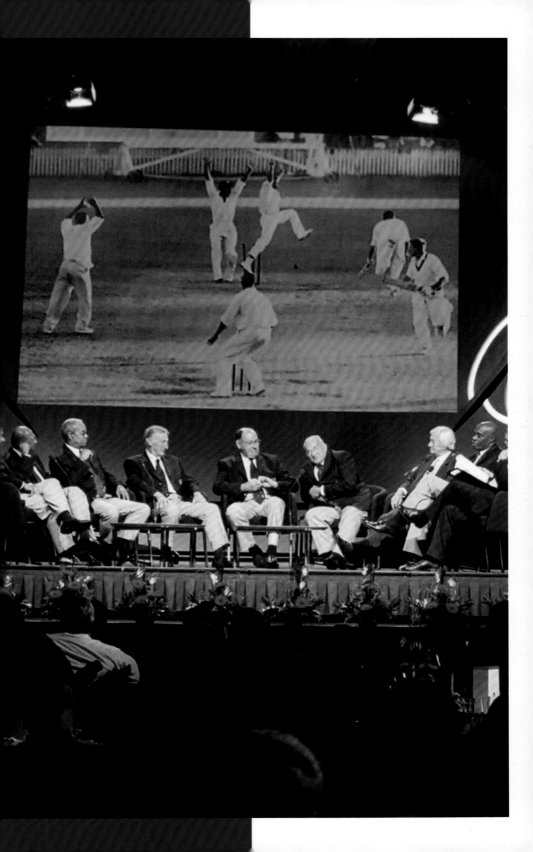

Most of the key tactical decisions made in a cricket match are made by the captain. They may consult with their teammates, coaches, statistical analysts and social media managers. But ultimately the final decision on the vast majority of tactical ploys comes down to the captain.

Which is why it's frustrating that we don't have better statistics for captaincy skills.

It's certainly theoretically *possible* to quantify the various aspects of captaincy, at least to some degree. With coin tosses, for example, we could measure the win–loss ratio of a captain in situations where they've won the toss. Then compare that to their win–loss ratio where they've lost the toss. Any differences between those numbers could be attributable to the decision made upon winning the toss. That's the first impact a captain has on a match, and the first one we might measure.

What about the quality of the field placements a captain employs? Well, that could, to some extent, be measured by examining the proportion of wickets taken by catches. (You'd exclude wicketkeeper catches from this calculation. Very few captains are bold enough to make the decision to move the wicketkeeper away from their usual position.) More catches taken suggests fielders have been placed in good positions.

Captains are also in charge of declarations. Those declarations are an attempt to change the balance of outcomes of a Test match. A declaration should increase the chances of the declaring team winning (*or* losing) the match. This is in exchange for decreasing their chances of *drawing* the match. By that logic, we could measure declaration timings by comparing the proportion of wins, draws and losses in those matches where a captain has declared.

And so on and so forth. For most decisions a captain makes, there is *some* way of measuring it. Which suggests it's possible to quantify whether the decisions made lead to the results for which the captain hoped. That's how, in an ideal world, a statistician would try to measure the skill of a captain.

However, the problem is that most of these calculations would be based on too small a sample size.

For example, a captain wins only half the tosses they take part in. (On average, that is; any skipper who wins appreciably more than this proportion has a completely different captaincy skill set.) Comparing the win–loss ratio between tosses won and tosses lost would too often be swamped by random fluctuations. Only the longest-term of leaders could hope to avoid this risk.

Declarations, to take another example, suggest that the team is in a strong position. There would be too few losses or draws from those positions to tease out any differences that could be attributed to their timing. Again, to make the numbers work, we'd need far more declarations than most captains are ever in a position to contemplate.

The proportion of catches is nice in theory. It indicates that fielders are in the correct position to take the chance. However, it also can't help but measure the number of chances the bowlers create. Which has little to do with captaincy.

These kind of weaknesses illustrate why such statistics will never catch on.

Instead, pretty much the only measure that's used is the win–loss ratio of teams under a captain's leadership. This is a terrible way of calculating captaincy prowess, since it's hopelessly entangled with the quality of players a leader happens to have in their team. But, hey, at least it's easy to calculate.

But maybe, just maybe, there's something to be gleaned from the unsatisfying attempts to quantify the skills of a captain. Maybe we should look at the win–loss measure, with all

its dependence on the quality of the captain's team, and accept the obvious conclusion: that *none* of a captain's tactical ploys has any meaningful impact on the result.

The tactics might be fun for fans of the game to debate and discuss. But the impact of a captain is *swamped* by whether they are leading a good cricket side or not.

However, if captains' tactical ploys – the declarations, the bowling changes, the nightwatchmen, the field placements and all the rest – are less important than the players who implement those ploys, what benefits, exactly, does a captain provide?

To answer that, let's go back to the 1960/61 Test series. Australia were chasing 233 in their final innings to win the first Test against the West Indies. At 6/92, with West Indies speedster Wes Hall blasting out the top order, the home side appeared doomed. But captain Richie Benaud and Alan Davidson saw Australia to tea at 6/109.

Donald Bradman, in his role as ACB chairman, approached Benaud during the tea break. Bradman was a captain renowned for the tactical cleverness of always having the greatest batter of all time as part of his team. He asked Benaud what he intended to do.

'Well, we're going for a win,' replied Benaud.

His response met with the Don's approval. Benaud and Davidson then proceeded to put on a record seventh-wicket partnership during the last session.

The pair took Australia to the brink of victory. However, with time running out in the match, Davidson was run out by Joe Solomon for 80, leaving Australia at 7/226. They were seven runs short of victory. One more run to round out the over left Australia on 7/227 with five minutes remaining. Wally Grout was on strike for what would prove to be the final eight-ball over of the match.

A scampered leg bye from the first ball reduced the runs required for victory to five. It also gave Benaud the strike. But not for long, as he was caught behind, completing a five-wicket Hall.

Suddenly, with Benaud and Davidson both gone, the West Indies were a mere two wickets from victory. They had six balls remaining and only Australia's bottom three batters to contend with.

A pair of missed chances from Hall – a run-out and a dropped catch – allowed Australia to reduce the target to three from the final three balls.

Ian Meckiff then swatted a ball deep to cow corner. The batters completed two runs, but Grout was run out going for the match-winning third. Australia needed one run to win. The West Indies needed one wicket. There were two balls left in the Test.

New batter Lindsay Kline pushed a quick single to the leg side. But it was too quick. Again, Solomon swooped in and threw down the stumps from side on to complete the run-out. Australia were all out. The scores were level. The Test was tied.

If we're thinking only about win–loss ratios, the tied Test had no impact on Benaud's record of captaincy. It was identical to what it would have been if Australia had instead batted out the final session for a draw.

But the first ever tied game of Test cricket shows where the true impact of captaincy can be felt. Not in the minor tactical tweaks to a match, which are trivial compared to the impact of the skills of the players. No, a captain's true impact transcends all the tactical fun. Instead, a captain defines the *mindset* of the team. This, in turn, defines how entertaining the cricket they play is.

That's an infinitely more important role.

NEXT:

More statistics! A look at how cricket deals with all the numbers at its core. Plus, winking meta-questions!

THE NUMBERS OF CRICKET

DON BRADMAN
SCORES A DUCK

Bradman

THE MOMENT:

As the 1948 Ashes draws to a conclusion, Don Bradman, playing his final Test and needing only four runs to finish with an average of 100, is bowled for a duck by Eric Hollies

During the 1980s, the board game Trivial Pursuit swept the game-playing world. It challenged pre–PlayStation era humans to answer general knowledge trivia questions. Those questions covered Geography, Entertainment, History, The Category for Which You Always Had to Rely on Wild Guesses, Science and Nature and Sports and Leisure.

And somewhere, hidden deep within the jam-packed boxes of trivia cards that came with the original edition of the game, was an astonishing Sports and Leisure question. A poser that would shake the preconceptions of even the most dogged of Trivial Pursuants:

'Which famous cricketer is the answer to this question?'

The answer, of course, was 'Donald Bradman'.

Trivial Pursuit was a board game not exactly renowned for its light-hearted whimsy. But it was able to indulge in such a winking meta-question because of Bradman's unparalleled dominance of the sport.

Indeed, the question itself evoked the spirit of Bradman: it was a bizarre outlier that transcended the commonplace and seemed to belong to a completely different game. The question was not just about Bradman, it embodied Bradman.

Other sports have their champions – the greats regarded as the best in their field. But none is as clear-cut as Bradman, who is cricket's finest wielder of the bat by absolute bloody miles. The top-notch batters in the history of Test cricket average 50 runs per innings. Beyond that greatness tier are a few exceptional legends. Players gifted with both the phenomenal hand-eye coordination and single-minded determination necessary to average in the vicinity of 60.

In most sports, that's where it ends, with a handful of all-time superstars operating at the peak of human ability. Fans of those other sports then get to argue over which of those transcendent legends is their choice as the best player. Sometimes, there's not even all that much debate. Despite the excellence of the others at the peak of the sport, there's one player who, by most agreed-upon measures, is a notch or two better. The greatest.

In cricket, we go beyond that. We top out at a batting average of 60 where the exceptional players loiter. And then look afield a further *forty* runs. And there we find Bradman, the utter lunatic, averaging near as dammit to 100.

(As always, all discussion on batting averages only includes those players with a substantial career record. This is to ensure we avoid the distorting

222

impact of brief, fluke careers. The definition for 'substantial career record' is usually either twenty innings or 2000 runs. The choice depends on how seriously the cricket statistician in question wants to take Adam Voges's career Test average of 61.87.)

Every now and then, people will offer up alternatives to Bradman as the greatest ever when it comes to batting. Such folk are invariably contrarians, click-baiters or mischief-makers. Crazy people willing to ignore the fact that statistics is an entire branch of actual mathematics. It comes with rigorous definitions and proofs and all the other guff that goes along with branches of mathematics. No, the gap between Bradman and the rest is so enormous that it's not even remotely possible that he is anything other than the best.

Having said that, it *is* justifiable to ignore Bradman from a certain statistical viewpoint. Imagine if the batting averages across the history of cricket were returned as the results of some scientific experiment. Any half-competent data scientist would immediately identify and discard the Bradman data point as an absurd outlier – an obvious experimental error that fails to fit with any reliable model for how we understand the sport.

And for the most part, that's how Bradman is treated. His nonsensical records are set aside for the freakish distractions they so self-evidently are. Instead, we frame most batting discussions in terms of 'the best since Bradman'.

Presumably, there's a 'best before Bradman' too. However, the vast majority of us are moving forward in time. (I'd insert a joke about *Tenet* here, were it not for the fact that I didn't understand a single thing that was going on in that movie.) As such, we tend not to focus too much on the pre-1928 side of the demarcation point.

In this way, we sidestep the tedium of comparing any other batter to Bradman. And avoid the inevitable mismatch that results.

Other great players, if they strike a rich enough vein of batting form, can sometimes match Bradman's standards for a summer or two. Fans and critics will then gush over their Bradmanesque feats over that period. And rightly so, because any sustained run of averaging triple figures is a phenomenal effort.

It's just that Bradman was Bradmanesque through most of his career. (The time he wasn't – the Bodyline series – he still averaged 56.57. Bradman's worst series was better than most players' best. Because he's Bradman and that's how numbers work around him.) It's Bradman's *sustained* preposterous excellence that renders him so incomparable.

Because of this, any time there's a cricket statistic that measures consistently high standards of batting, you can be confident that Bradman will pop up in the corresponding table.

As a random example, the table for the least number of innings to reach 5000 Test runs. This list has all-time greats such as Garfield Sobers, Viv Richards, Len Hutton, Sachin Tendulkar, Brian Lara, Sunil Gavaskar and Steve Smith. Those champion batters all reached the tally in roughly a hundred innings. The remarkable Jack Hobbs managed to amass the milestone in a mere ninety-one innings.

Bradman took fifty-six.

Yet there's nothing unique about Bradman's dominance of that particular statistical table. He dominates *all* such tables. If there were a statistic for the number of batting record statistics dominated by an individual player, Bradman would dominate that one too.

His batting standard ruins all-rounder statistics too. One common method for measuring all-rounder quality is batting average minus bowling average. But Bradman tops that list too.

Bradman's numbers ruin *everything*.

Which is why the greatest thing about Bradman is actually his final innings. The duck that meant he finished with an average of 99.94.

Cricket is a magnificent sport for many reasons. One of those reasons is how funny it is. Nonsense happens so often in cricket that it must surely be built into the sport's very fabric, in ways we don't yet fully understand.

To build up a near-mythical superhuman over the course of two decades, having him perform unimaginable feats beyond the scope of any of his teammates or opponents, in the process amassing an unsurpassable record, is one thing. To punchline that demigod's entire career with the lowest possible score in his last time at bat is quite another.

But of course, even such a comical twist ending to a career can be tempered with a mind-boggling Bradman statistic. Crunching the numbers, it turns out that Bradman could have made a further *forty* ducks at the back end of his career and still had a better Test average than any other player in the history of the game.

A thoroughly ludicrous individual. That's how you get your name into a Trivial Pursuit trick question.

NEXT:

A mortal batter matches Bradman on one particular table. Off the last ball of the day. Plus, crowds of velociraptors!

STEVE WAUGH HITS A FOUR

Centuries

THE MOMENT:

In the fifth and final Test of the 2002/03 summer, Australian captain Steve Waugh brings up a century and saves his career by hitting the last ball of the day for four

Non-cricket fans must have been annoyed beyond all measure. The news was an unfathomable forty-five minutes late. Channel Nine screens remained stubbornly on the cricket. Those of us sensible enough to be fans of cricket knew that the rest of the news could wait. What was going on at the SCG was the only news story that mattered.

All summer, Australian captain Steve Waugh had been batting poorly, albeit on an upward trend. He'd started with 7 and 12 at the Gabba. Then followed it with 34 at Adelaide and 53 at Perth, as Australia secured the Ashes with minimal effort.

At Melbourne for the Boxing Day Test, he'd looked even better, amassing a fine 77 in the first innings before being caught behind. Then, in the second innings, he'd looked far, far worse. Lost in the middle during an absurd knock. One in which he was caught behind but not given out because England didn't bother to appeal. Then caught at short extra cover but not given out because of a no ball. Then actually caught and out for a hideous 14. It was a shambolic innings from the migraine-suffering Waugh. The sole comfort for his fans was that the England side was, as ever, even more of a shambles.

But Waugh's awful innings had not gone unnoticed by the eagle-eyed chairman of selectors, Trevor Hohns. Any upward trend in Waugh's batting had been forgotten. In Sydney, the fifth and final Test of the summer, the Australian captain would be batting for his career.

And so, on the second day of the Test, with Australia on 3/56 in reply to England's first innings of 362, Waugh raced to the crease. An adoring SCG crowd gave him a standing ovation all the way to the middle.

Y'know, just in case.

But Waugh wasn't there for 'thanks for the memories' applause. Waugh still had memories to make.

He got off the mark with a clip off his pads that raced to the boundary. The timing was good. It stayed good as he ticked his way through the runs. Entering the scheduled final hour of the day, he brought up his fifty with a cover drive for four. Shortly after, having been joined by Adam Gilchrist, he cut a ball for four to bring up 10,000 Test runs, becoming only the third man to do so.

He'd made his way to 80 by the time Nine were due to go to their scheduled news coverage. Instead, Tony Greig informed viewers that they would be staying with the cricket until Waugh got his hundred. Or got out. Waugh and Gilchrist then combined to give fans the maximum amount of cricket possible. Sorry, news junkies.

First, Gilchrist managed to take the strike for several overs. Then Waugh, with two overs to go, decided to go for the ton.

He sliced a four to go from 88 to 92, then ran a two that was best described as ambitious, diving his way home to go to 94. A single gave him 95 and the strike for the final over.

A three with three balls remaining moved Waugh to 98. Then, off the day's penultimate delivery, Gilchrist returned the strike to his skipper with a raucously-cheered single.

Waugh had the strike for the final ball of the day.

England captain Nasser Hussain dragged out the moment, talking to bowler Richard Dawson at length, as he rearranged the field.

But finally, inevitably, famously, Waugh pounced on the final delivery. He smoked it through the covers, jumping in the air with delight as he moved to 102. In addition to saving his career, he'd equalled Sir Donald Bradman as the Australian with the most Test centuries. The SCG rocked in delight, with every person at the ground standing and applauding Waugh as he departed the ground at the close of play.

Finally, Nine could go to the news. A news telecast that led with the story of Waugh's ton.

Waugh's desperation to reach his century before stumps makes no actual sporting sense, of course. If he'd finished the day on 98, the difference to the match would have been negligible, a mere 1.6 per cent fewer runs to Australia's innings at that point.

The century as a landmark doesn't even make any sense from a mathematical point of view. There's nothing intrinsically special about a score of 100. Its sole significance is that it represents the addition of an extra digit to the recording of the score. But that extra digit exists only in our usual base-10 counting system. Which in turn arises only from the evolutionary fluke of us having ten fingers (assuming thumbs can be considered a variant of fingers). If humans had a different number of fingers, different cricket landmarks would be recognised. (Also, batting gloves would need a radical redesign.)

As a quick recap, base-10 arithmetic revolves around the numbers we get from our usual ten digits: 0, 1, 2, 3, 4, 5, 6, 7, 8 and 9. Once you get past nine, you start building two-digit numbers such as, say, 47 (eventually). In the number 47, the '4' represents the number of tens and the '7' the number of units, giving us a total of 40 + 7 = 47. At this stage, not particularly edifying or counterintuitive, I'll grant you. And, of course, in base-10, we run out of two-digit numbers once we go past 99. Which is when we add a third digit – to the ecstatic cheers of the SCG crowd.

If we only had eight digits, however (0, 1, 2, 3, 4, 5, 6 and 7), things would be different. We'd run out of single-digit numbers when we reached what we usually call 8. With no 8 in our set of digits, we have to start our two-digit numbers earlier. So, 10 in base-8 represents what we'd ordinarily call 8. A 47 in base-8 would have the '4' representing the number of 8s and the '7' representing the number of units, giving us a number equivalent to what in base-10 is 39 (or 4 x 8 + 7). (Yeah, not so trivial now, is it? That'll teach you to get cocky with your maths.)

In base-8, the three figures of 100 would represent a score of what we usually think of as 64. A century in a universe of four-fingered people (such as *The Simpsons*) is a decent score, to be sure. But it's not quite as worthy of frenzied cheering.

In this *Simpsons* cricketing universe, it's Steve Smith who averages close to 100. (Bradman averages almost 144.) *Simpsons* Allan Border would have retired shortly after becoming the first batter in the history of Test cricket to reach a century of centuries (64 scores of 64 or higher). Poor old *Simpsons* Sunil Gavaskar fell one short of that tally. D'oh!

And *Simpsons* Steve Waugh would have broken that record in this innings. Not off the last ball, of course, but it still would have had the crowd on their eight-toed feet, for sure. Maybe that was destined to happen in all universes.

What about a universe of three-fingered cricketers? Say, ones that had evolved from velociraptors. Now, we're working in base-6, in which we reach centuries for scoring a mere 36 of our base-10 runs.

Hardly worth getting worked up about, is it? If every half-decent Test batter is averaging better than a century, then what are we even doing here?

Perhaps, then, the landmark for our velocicricketers wouldn't be three figures. Four figures would make more sense. For a base-6 1000 is equal to 216 of our normal base-10 runs.

And if *that* was the accepted benchmark for a great innings, then our old friend Donald Bradlizard remains at the top of the list of most Test thousands, and unlikely to ever be challenged. Certainly not by Steve Waughosaurus, still stuck on zero Test thousands.

You can bet the lizards would have got their news on time that day.

NEXT:

How do we best rank cricketers? Or teams of cricketers? Plus, ladder yo-yos!

MARK TAYLOR CLAIMS THE SIR FRANK WORRELL TROPHY

Rankings

THE MOMENT:

Australia win the fourth and final Test of the 1995 series against the West Indies to inflict the first defeat on them in fifteen years

A stunned West Indies captain Richie Richardson couldn't believe it. He'd had a rest day between the third and fourth days of the Test to get used to the idea, but it still hadn't sunk in.

At stumps on the third day, the West Indies were 3/63, still 203 runs away from making Australia bat again. Steve Waugh's double-century in Australia's first innings had ground them down. Paul Reiffel had backed that up with three early wickets, including Richardson himself and the great Brian Lara for a duck. (The Lara wicket had been a dire LBW decision that future umpire Paul Reiffel admitted he'd never give out. Didn't stop him from appealing, though.)

When the sides reconvened the Test after the rest day, Australia mopped up the remaining West Indies wickets. Glenn McGrath and Reiffel picked up a wicket apiece, before Shane Warne wrapped up the tail. When he caught the edge of number eleven Kenny Benjamin's bat, with captain Mark Taylor taking the catch at first slip, the match was done. Australia had won by an innings and 53 runs.

The series tally was 2–1 to Taylor's men. It was the first series loss for the West Indies in fifteen years. It meant the Sir Frank Worrell Trophy was in Australian hands for the first time since 1978. Australia could now lay claim to being the best team in the world.

But the West Indies weren't giving up the throne so easily. Sure, they'd lost the Test series. But they hadn't yet lost the argument about what it meant about who was the best team in the world.

Richie Richardson began the debate with a muddled post-match argument. 'I can't believe we lost to Australia,' he said. He added that it was 'the weakest Australian side I've played against'.

To be fair, his comments came in the aftermath of the first series defeat any of the West Indies players had ever experienced. So we can forgive Richardson if it came across as both (a) ungracious and (b) implying that his own side was the weakest West Indies side in which he'd ever played.

But even if what Richardson was saying was true, it didn't *necessarily* mean that the West Indies weren't still the best side in the world. Was one series defeat enough to cost them that title? That was debatable. And it was to the West Indies' enormous credit that the debate hadn't existed for a decade and a half. Such had been their unparalleled dominance.

After this 1995 series, there was a brief interim period where debate over which side was the best Test team was justified. But continued success soon saw Australia accepted as the new top team in the world. It was then their turn to put the debate to bed for another decade or so, with their own era of indomitability.

But Australia's defeat in the 2005 Ashes opened the door again for further questioning. Coincidentally, or otherwise, this was when the ICC first released its official rankings.

The ranking system was complicated, but it more or less had to be. Test match series were a hodgepodge. They were scattered indiscriminately across the calendar. Teams, at best, faced off against one another only once every two years or so. To bring any kind of mathematical sense to a ranking system was a challenge.

At least with ODIs (and later T20 internationals), there were regular World Cups. Somebody could always claim to be the champion, and if the ranking system threw up quirks, it didn't matter so much. The World Cup champions were an easy fallback position.

Test cricket didn't have that. Oh, sure, there had been attempts to have World Test championships over the years. But the commonplace nature of drawn matches made it a difficult tournament to wrap one's head around. And so the ICC tended to completely

unwrap their heads from any promised Test championships. On multiple occasions, the entire concept was aborted at the slightest provocation.

(In a strange twist, the World Test championship format that stuck long enough to get to a final was the one that took place between 2019 and 2021. This was despite genuine reasons for having second thoughts. Such as a convoluted points system that inexplicably rewarded teams that played shorter series. Or a mid-tournament points-scoring recalibration. Oh, and a global pandemic that saw multiple tours abandoned.)

But before that, all Test cricket had were the rankings.

The rankings had, and have, flaws. The main one is that they're always out of date, since they average results over a few years. They *have* to do that, though. You can't have rankings depend on the single most recent Test a nation has played. At least, not without plenty of yo-yoing up and down the ladder with any upset win or loss. (Kids: never yo-yo on ladders.)

There are other problems with how the ICC calculates the rankings — most notably, a lack of discrimination between home and away results. Overall, the various flaws mean the rankings are rarely better than fine. They anoint a number-one team, but inspire little confidence in that lionisation.

Indeed, the great irony of the ICC rankings is that the only times they're widely accepted come when one team is so far ahead of the rest that the rankings are superfluous anyway.

This is also true of the individual player rankings, which are calculated with an algorithm that is somehow even more complicated. If, for example, somebody is the number-one ranked batter for seventeen years, then you probably don't need an algorithm to tell you that. (You know who I'm talking about. Short guy. Right-handed. Averaged forty more runs than anybody else.)

The rest of the time, there are sufficient flaws to enable arguments to continue about the relative merits of teams or players. Those arguments can contain all the usual number-fudging that a certain kind of cricket fan lives for.

'How can India be number one when they lost to England at home?'

'How can England be number one when they don't even have the Ashes?'

'How can Australia be number one when they were thrashed by India?'

'Um, excuse me. We're New Zealand and we kind of, uh, keep winning?'

'Shush.'

And round and round it goes. Most of the confusion can be traced back to the West Indies and Australian sides. The ones that were so dominant they rendered rankings superfluous. The outstanding quality of those sides means that many fans still tend to equate 'number-one side' with 'all-time great side'.

But that's not necessary. The number-one ranked side doesn't have to be particularly good in a historical context. They just have to be the best side against the other nations at a particular point in time. You could even be the worst Australian side against which Richie Richardson ever played, or the worst West Indies side in which Richie Richardson ever played, and *still* be the number-one side. As long as all the other sides were worse.

But which was it? Fortunately, the ICC have back-calculated the rankings using their now-standard methodology. This allows us to answer the question of which of these two puny sides was officially superior when Australia defeated the West Indies in 1995.

According to the rankings at the time, the two sides were almost impossible to split, with both on 112 points. Although the West Indies still had the edge when the numbers were measured to an extra decimal place. Four months later, however, the West Indies were officially toppled from the number-one spot in the ICC rankings – and they never regained it.

That new number-one Test team in September 1995 was, of course . . . uh, India?

Oh, ICC rankings. You're so crazy.

NEXT:

Even when the West Indies lost their number-one team ranking, they still contained the number-one batter. On multiple measures. Plus, uninterested security guards!

BRIAN LARA SCORES 375

Records

THE MOMENT:

In the fifth Test against England in 1994, West Indies champion batter Brian Lara breaks the world record score for most runs in an individual innings

For a little over thirty-six years, the highest individual Test score was held by Garfield Sobers. His 365 not out in a total of 3/790 declared against Pakistan in 1958 seemed a perfect kind of total to hold the record. A run for every day of the year, and still not out to pick up the bonus run in a leap year.

The record had steadily progressed from Charles Bannerman's 165 not out, increasing by an extra couple of hundred runs over the first eighty-one years of Test cricket.

Australia's Billy Murdoch had been the first to take the record, with the first double-century, in 1884. Reginald Foster, known as 'Tip' for his enthusiasm in putting rubbish away, claimed the record for England in 1903, when he scored 287.

Fellow Englishman Andy Sandham made the first Test triple-century, in April 1930, boosting the record to 325. Then the old show-off Bradman decided to poke his head into yet another record book. In August 1930, he scored a triple-century in one day on his way to 334.

The record was back in English hands three years later, when Wally Hammond made 336 not out, before Len Hutton extended the mark to 364 in 1938. Hutton held the record for almost twenty years before Sobers went past him in 1958, claiming it for the West Indies for the first time.

And there the record stayed. Until Brian Lara came along.

There are all manner of cricketing records that can be tallied. In any given match, broadcasters have paid statisticians keeping an eye out for obscure landmarks that might be surpassed.

The highest score by a number eight in Australia v Pakistan Test matches at the SCG? (Sarfaraz Ahmed, 72 not out, 2017.) Highest fifth-wicket partnership in a loss in India? (Michael Clarke and Matthew Wade, 145, in 2013.) Most catches in an innings by a non-English non-wicketkeeper at Lord's? (Our man Sobers again, with four in 1973.)

The records that capture the most interest, however, tend to be batting ones. Yes, when a bowler takes a five-wicket haul they'll hold the ball up to the crowd to mark the moment. But the problem for bowlers is simply a lack of range. And a lack of gradation within that range. Even if you search for esoteric records for number of wickets captured in an innings, you'll still see a lot of tied results. Skilful statisticians can delve into all kinds of obscure criteria for a record. But even so, it's difficult to track down instances where a bowler gets to outright hold a record for a number of wickets.

Heck, even the record for the absolute maximum – ten wickets in an innings – is shared by Jim Laker and Anil Kumble.

To split records of bowlers who've tied for the most wickets in an innings, we look to the number of runs conceded in taking those wickets. This only accentuates the point that runs are a more nuanced measurement for cricket records.

The only way around this fundamental problem for bowlers is to look at *career* records. And, to be fair, when some kind of record for the most career wickets is breached, that's generally celebrated widely. (Never in more tongue-in-cheek fashion than when Nathan Lyon surpassed Hugh Trumble's career record of 141 Test wickets as an Australian off-spinner, and was promptly nicknamed the GOAT (Greatest Of All Time) as a result.)

But the problem with career records is that you can see them coming. Because they're cumulative, it's usually obvious from a long way out that a player is closing in on a record. Anybody with even a passing interest can count down to the moment when it's broken.

An individual record in an innings, or a Test – or heck, maybe even a series – is different. Players start from zero at the beginning, which means there's no heads-up several Tests out that a player's getting close to the record. Any individual record could be broken in the very next Test you watch.

That's exactly what happened in April 1994. West Indies won the toss and chose to bat first. It was a decision they might have regretted when they lost both openers with just 12 runs on the board. But the West Indies in 1994 were still the best team in the world. And one of the reasons was that they had Brian Charles Lara, an all-time great at the peak of his form.

A year earlier, he'd made his first Test century, an epic 277 against Australia in only his fifth Test. Two months later, he would head over to England and break the record first-class score by striking 501 not out for Warwickshire against Durham.

In between the debut double-ton and the first-class score of half a thousand runs, Lara settled for breaking Sobers's Test record.

Over a series of double-century-ish partnerships with Jimmy Adams (179 runs), Keith Arthurton (183) and Shivnarine Chanderpaul (219), Lara made his way towards Sobers's mark. He went past it by pulling a short ball to the boundary. He punched the air with sufficient delight to spin himself completely around. The crowd surged onto the field, avoiding the security guards stationed to stop them. (Not a big challenge. The guards were, in the words of commentator Michael Holding, 'just happy to be so close to Brian Lara, not too interested in getting the crowd off the field.')

Lara hugged Chanderpaul. Sobers, who had been nervously waiting at the boundary edge, strode onto the ground for his own embrace. He beamed as he congratulated the man who'd broken his record.

Lara was out six runs later for 375. Nobody cared. The record had been broken. (The Test itself petered out to a draw, with England precisely matching the West Indies' 5/593 declared with 593 runs of their own.)

Lara held his 375 record for a decade, until Matthew Hayden decided to beat up on Zimbabwe and Steve Waugh refused to step in and stop him. Hayden scored 380 against the hapless side. In the process, he went past the Australia record of 334 shared by Bradman and Mark Taylor, the latter of whom had famously declared the innings closed before he could surpass the score.

While Lara wasn't at the ground to honour Hayden in person, he called him to offer congratulations. Then Lara took the record back six months later, hitting the first ever Test *quadruple*-century when he made 400 not out against England at the same ground where he'd hit 375 ten years earlier.

Lara therefore holds the record for the most times an individual has held the record for the highest individual Test score. With two (2).

NEXT:

Sobers performs other rousing batting feats. One that's even tougher to surpass. Plus, the infinite nature of the cosmos!

GARFIELD SOBERS

HITS SIX SIXES IN AN OVER

Six Sixes

THE MOMENT:

During an England county championship match in 1968, Nottinghamshire captain Garfield Sobers hits Glamorgan spinner Malcolm Nash for six sixes in one over

In mathematical terms, 36 has a number of qualities going for it. It's a triangular number, being the sum of the first eight integers. It's the atomic number of krypton, the key element in green, red *and* gold kryptonite, which respectively kill, mutate and permanently depower Kryptonians. It's the ASCII code for the dollar sign and, hence, the shirt number of multimillionaire Australian Test captain Tim Paine. And, of course, it is six squared.

It's this last fact that gives 36 its great power in cricket. For six is both the number of balls in a typical over, as well as the maximum number of runs typically available from a cricket shot. Which means that, in a typical unfolding of the cricketing world, 36 is the highest number of runs one can score from a single over.

The word 'typical' is working overtime in that previous paragraph. That's because there are several *a*typical mechanisms by which both the number of balls in an over and the maximum number of runs from a ball can exceed six.

The first isn't even all *that* atypical. It only takes a no ball or wide for an over to be more than six balls long. This is something that fans see with such regularity it's not worth commenting on. In this, it's much like batters being given a drink outside of the scheduled breaks. Or Meg Lanning scoring an ODI century.

Further along the atypical spectrum, seven can be scored from a single ball. All it takes is one careless overthrow at an inappropriate moment. Indeed, there is no *actual* limit to the number of runs that can be scored from one delivery. A series of wild flings at the stumps or the ball being swallowed by a deep fine leg fielder could lead to any number of runs being scored. In theory, at least.

So there are caveats on each of the upper limits of these two key factors. Despite this, 36 is still perceived as the maximum number of runs that can be achieved from a single over.

This is despite the existence of a 43-run over in New Zealand domestic List A cricket as recently as 2018. Joe Carter and Brett Hampton of Northern Districts reacted to an over from Willem Ludick with the following: 4, 6+nb, 6+nb, 6, 1, 6, 6, 6.

But let's set aside the batting heroics of New Zealand domestic cricketers. For a moment. There remain a couple of reasons why it's so comforting to think of 36 as a maximum, despite it being definitively not so.

Firstly, it's easy to envisage. We have seen all manner of batters hit all manner of sixes. To contemplate the possibility of a 36-run over requires only that one imagine such a blow six times in succession. And while this is an unlikely thing to take place, it's aided by a pleasing simplicity to the entire concept. It doesn't matter where each six goes. It can be tonked over cow corner. It can be sliced over that dunderwhelp at deep third man. It can be helicopter-shot into the crowd. But at its heart it's the same bowler (ideally, Stuart Broad) being hit by the same batter (say, Yuvraj Singh in 2007) for the same score, six times in a row. In information theory terms, it's a concept of low complexity (see also: Warner, David).

Garfield Sobers did it. Then Ravi Shastri did it. Herschelle Gibbs, Yuvraj Singh, Hazratullah Zazai, Kieron Pollard, Thisara Perera and others all did it. So 36 runs in an over is almost no big deal these days.

To score more than 36 in an over, on the other hand, requires a series of Lemony Snicketesque unfortunate events. Some sixes, sure, but also some no balls, some wides, some overthrows and Lord's only knows what else. These different outcomes can take place in a variety of orders, and with either batter on strike. It's therefore a concept of higher information complexity than the simple six sixes. That's what makes it harder for us to imagine.

As such, even though both outcomes are of infinitesimal likelihood, the 36 *feels* like it's more of a barrier. It acts as a threshold, not because it represents any kind of limit in a mathematical sense, but more because it represents a limit in a conceptual sense.

There's another advantage to thinking of 36 as an upper limit to run-scoring from an over. Even the most conservative of fielding captains will see a required run rate of 36 in a limited-overs match as a point where they can relax. It's the moment when an otherwise remorseless defence can give way to crowd-pleasing bowling changes. When a skipper might toss the ball to a retiring, inebriated or otherwise beloved player to roll their arm over for the benefit of an adoring crowd.

Of course, the difference here is that to concede more than 36 runs in an over is only possible if the bowler is distracted by other goals. For example, an attempt to take wickets or, paradoxically, to limit the number of runs being scored. In such a case, the bowler exerts extra effort in straining for these alternative objectives. This can lead to the no balls or wides that are the building blocks upon which an over in excess of 36 can be built.

In contrast, a bowler with the sole goal of keeping the scoring to 36 or below from a given over need not strain themselves. They are seemingly in complete control of securing this achievement. All they need to do is land their foot behind the crease, pitch the ball in line with the batter (without beaming them or bending their arm) and have fielders run the ball back to the keeper. This is considered trivial enough that there's zero risk of failure. Which, again, is not quite accurate. Especially since the type of players for whom one needs a 36-run buffer before contemplating throwing them the ball are the ones most likely to mess up the basics of bowling.

Nevertheless, the perception of 36 as the maximum is a conceit that both captains and fans are willing to embrace. Because the alternative is to revert to facing the reality that there is *no* limit to the runs that can be scored from an over. To stare into the infinite abyss of the long tail of low-probability events and wonder 'what if?'.

That way lies madness. And this is also what makes 36 a near-perfect microcosm of how humanity as a whole understands the infinite cosmos and our place in it.

Humans can't properly understand the vastness of the universe. Instead, we filter the unbounded enormity of the cosmos through our limited sensory organs. Shrinking the infinite down to something large but understandable just makes things simpler.

Oh, and speaking of concepts that tame the incomprehensible and reframe it as something that we, as mortals, can comprehend: 36 is also the perfectly mediocre Test bowling average of Donald Bradman.

Honestly, you can't get rid of him from any discussion about cricketing numbers.

NEXT:

36 is one of cricket's best numbers. But which is the worst? Plus, cut-price Draculas!

SHANE WARNE
IS OUT FOR 99

Unlucky Numbers

THE MOMENT:

In the third Test against New Zealand in 2001/02, Shane Warne is caught in the deep for 99

As Batman taught us in the issue outlining his secret origin in *Detective Comics 27* in 1939, cricketers are a superstitious, cowardly lot. No, wait. That's criminals. *Criminals* are a superstitious, cowardly lot. Which is all the justification that Bruce Wayne needs to dress up like a cut-price Dracula before heading out to beat them to a pulp.

Cricketers, as a rule, are not noticeably chickenhearted. Nor do they tend to be the targets of a billionaire vigilante deep in the 'anger' stage of grief. They are, however, deeply superstitious.

As we've seen, batters accord special meaning to certain numbers of runs based solely on the number of digits those scores contain in a base-10 counting system. It's no surprise, then, that those same cricketers might also perceive other numbers of runs as unlucky.

In Australia, it's 87 that's deemed an unlucky cricketing number, because it's 13 short of a century. England, on the other hand, claim that 111, known as 'Nelson' (after the *Simpsons* character, one imagines) is an unlucky number. This is because the three ones resemble a wicket with no bails on it. If an English batter falls for 111, they're 'Ha-ha!'ed off the ground.

Of course, if you asked most batters which score would irritate them more, approximately 100 per cent of them would choose 87 over 111. Because, y'know, the latter is 24 runs more than the former. So where England get off claiming that 111 is an unlucky score is beyond me.

Even if we accept that superstitions don't need to make sense, there are, however, only two real candidates for the unluckiest score. There's zero, the mathematically endorsed candidate, the official lowest tally a batter can score. (We'll get to that unlucky number very soon indeed.) And then there's 99, the score where a batter falls a run short of the accepted landmark score.

Any dismissal in the 'nervous nineties' is considered unfortunate. The kind of innings that demands the balm of 'deserved a hundred' commiserations. And no score 'deserves a hundred' more than 99. Other than any score where a hundred was actually achieved, of course. (Bradman, unsurprisingly, didn't do scores in the nineties. If he deserved a hundred, he went and bloody well scored one. Nerves are for other, more human cricketers.)

But of all the 99s in the history of Test cricket, it's hard to come up with one unluckier than Shane Warne's in 2001.

Australia were at the peak of their Test cricket prowess at this time, swatting aside every nation that dared oppose them. Yes, they'd stumbled in India, succumbing to one of the great Test (and series) comebacks. But since then they'd gone to England and rampaged their way through there. They dropped just the one Test after a generous declaration in search of a clean sweep, and a once-in-a-lifetime innings of 173 not out by Mark Butcher.

Back in Australia at the beginning of the 2001/02 summer, however, Stephen Fleming's New Zealand team had tactically outmanoeuvred the Australians. Not enough to beat them – tactics, as we've seen, can only take a team so far. But a combination of rain and well-executed bowling plans had seen the first two Tests of the series drawn.

The third Test would therefore decide the series. Fleming won the toss and made the tactically astute decision to bat on a flat WACA pitch. His batters then piled on enormous, tactical runs. With four centuries in the innings, they declared late on the second day at 9/534, taking the wicket of Matthew Hayden before stumps.

On the third day, the Australian batters continued to fall. When Adam Gilchrist was out with the score at 6/192, there was a real risk that Australia would be forced to follow on. And a real risk they'd then lose a Test series at home for the first time in almost a decade. Little New Zealand were taking on arguably the greatest Test team ever assembled – Hayden, Langer, Ponting, Mark and Steve Waugh, Martyn, Gilchrist, Warne, Lee, Gillespie and McGrath – and dominating them.

The wicket of Gilchrist brought Warne to the crease. Nobody was more excited by this than the fan in the crowd wearing a T-shirt that read 'Warney's Grouse at Cricket'. The great leg-spinner was not about to make that T-shirt a liar. He and Damien Martyn immediately counterattacked. Martyn did that thing where he exquisitely timed everything with the barest of movements. Warne, meanwhile, thrashed and pulled and grunted. Both techniques worked well, and the pair added 78 for the seventh wicket before Martyn was tactically caught by Fleming, slashing to gully.

The loss of Martyn didn't deter Warne, who continued to bat without fear. He brought up his half-century off 94 balls, with seven boundaries. He then accelerated further, with his next 48 runs coming off 63 balls. The loss of both Brett Lee and Jason Gillespie at the other end deterred him not one iota.

With last man Glenn McGrath in, the threat of the follow-on countered, and his score on 99, Warne found a delivery from Daniel Vettori in his slot. He got under it, lofting it deep into the leg side. Through his entire innings, he'd found success with aerial shots. But this one would be his undoing.

Mark Richardson zoomed in to take the catch, then turned to the crowd with a theatrical bow. The man in the 'Warney's Grouse at Cricket' shirt blew his top. And the grouse-at-cricketer himself trudged off the ground, furious that he'd fallen one run short of the milestone.

The rest of the Test was a mini-classic of its own. In their second innings, New Zealand sprinted their way to 9/256 to set Australia 440 with a little under four sessions remaining.

On the final day, Australia were 5/244 with 28 overs still remaining and the new ball due, when Gilchrist joined Steve Waugh. The pair first saw off the threat of the new ball. They then guided Australia to 5/299 and the safety of a draw with less than an hour of play remaining. Phew!

At that point, however, Gilchrist decided he'd quite like to take a shot at scoring the 141 runs needed from the last 13 overs – if that was all right with the captain? Waugh gave him the nod, and Gilchrist launched an 18-run barrage of an over against Vettori. Then added another 14 runs in the next over, once Waugh gave him the strike against Chris Cairns. In a flash, he'd reduced the target to 108 off 11 overs.

It had taken two overs of power Gilchrist hitting to turn everybody's perception of the Test on its head.

It took only one more power shot to turn it back off its head again. That's when a straight drive off Vettori clipped the bowler's fingers and hit the stumps at the non-striker's end, running out Waugh. Gilchrist reluctantly abandoned the chase. He changed down his formidable gears to once again settle for the draw, as the luckless Waugh departed.

But Waugh's misfortune didn't compare to Warne's 99, especially as more information came to light.

Warne would never score a Test century. He finished his career with 3154 runs, almost a thousand runs clear of the next highest non-century-scorer.

Scoring over 3000 Test runs without once cracking three figures might make a batter feel cursed. That curse would sting further, however, with the later revelation that Vettori overstepped on the wicket-taking delivery. (Do curses sting? Let's say they do.)

So Warne's best chance at making his sole century had been undone by a no ball that the umpire didn't spot. Worse still, Warne *knew* he would have scored his century if the no ball *had* been called. This wasn't a case of him still having to find a scoring shot to bring up the milestone. Warne could have completed his ton while the ball was still in the air, heading out to Richardson.

Now, *that's* proper unluckiness.

Warney's grouse at being dismissed for the unluckiest 99 in the history of the game.

NEXT:

The actual unluckiest cricket number. Time to duck. Plus, wishy-washy masochism!

ALLAN DONALD DOESN'T RUN

Ducks

THE MOMENT:

With scores level in the 1999 World Cup semi-final between Australia and South Africa, Allan Donald remains at the non-striker's end for too long and is run out

Ducks make cricket great.

Oh, sure, there will be some who say that a superior method for dealing with a short ball is to sway away from it. To keep a wary eye on its trajectory, even as you bend further and further away, like a teenage girl negotiating the greeting kiss of a too affectionate uncle she's meeting for the first time. Sways work well, right up until the moment you realise it's still coming at you and you can sway no further.

There are other batters who don't look to avoid the bouncer at all. They prefer to counter-attack any bowler who has the temerity to drop the ball short in their vicinity. Pull shots and hook shots are plucked from these batters' repertoires with breathless abandon and thrown into battle. It's a dangerous ploy. Such an escalation in hostilities may sometimes win you the 2005 Ashes. But it's just as likely to see you caught in the deep like an idiot.

Then there are those strange batters who don't strive for avoidance, or who respond with hostility of their own. Batters who weigh up their 'flight or fight' options, decide instead to add an 'n' to the middle word, and allow the ball to strike them on the body. This kind of wishy-washy masochism is no good to anybody.

So for mine, it's the duck that is the best response to the bouncer. A blend of basic knee joint functionality and the gravitational constant G. It gets the batter swiftly and safely under the rising ball. The bouncer goes up, the batter goes down. Nothing simpler.

Yes, sometimes ducks can go wrong. A batter might be foolish enough to leave their bat periscoping in the air for a stray deflection to a nearby fielder. Or they might misjudge the bounce to such a degree that even at maximum downscrunch, they're still struck on the shoulder in front of the stumps and given out LBW. (Glenn McGrath once dismissed Sachin Tendulkar in this fashion. In retrospect, it's a tad miraculous that India didn't immediately refuse to use the LBW law for a decade.)

But all in all, ducks have a lot of things going for them.

So, let's get into it, then. Ducks. What are they? How should batters best use them? Why is it the best method of short-ball avoidance?

Ha ha ha.

No. As you've no doubt realised by now, this entire preamble has been a bit of silly mock-confusion. A few paragraphs of homonym-exploitation to open the piece.

We're not talking about batters ducking under bouncers. We are, instead, talking about nothing.

Because I am, of course, referring to 'ducks' in the cricketing sense of a runless innings. For just as the invention of zero was one of the most important breakthroughs in mathematics, the duck is one of the greatest aspects of cricket.

In an era of T20s and big bats, with runs being clobbered hither and yon (and vice versa), it's easy to get carried away with the idea of batters. To marvel at their outrageous array of shots, their split-second reflexes or their brute, physical power.

And yet, as bowlers remain keen to always remind us, batters aren't, to quote the younglings, all that.

The score of zero – the noble duck – remains by far the most common tally to be 'achieved' throughout the history of cricket. Yes, as we'll discuss shortly, some of this is due to cricket having the sublime feature of elite bowlers bowling to decidedly non-elite batters. But even in more balanced encounters, ducks are still surprisingly prevalent.

Ducks happen roughly 8–9 per cent of the time to top-order batters. To put that another way, approximately one-twelfth of the time, the best batters in the cricket world do no better than a random person plucked from the street (for example, Kelly Clarkson). Or, to put it still another way, if top-order batters batted once a day for a year, they would spend an entire month being dismissed for a hapless duck.

It's easy to overlook how strange this is, because we're so used to it. These same batters soon become so fluent at the crease, with runs flowing so effortlessly, that they can tally a hundred or more of the ruddy things before being dismissed.

And yet that first run, to avoid the duck, is inordinately trickier to negotiate.

What a wonderful aspect of a sport. To have a player's participation in their key skill set cut short at the first mistake. And then have that first mistake be so much more likely to occur earlier rather than later. Any success achieved with the bat must be that much sweeter for knowing it comes in such a ruthless sport. One biased towards duckly failure.

In a vain attempt to temper this horror of the duck-based spectre looming over them like an impenetrable *Far Side* cartoon, batters have given certain variants of ducks cutesy nicknames. There are golden ducks, where a batter is dismissed from the first ball faced. There are also platinum ducks.

And royal ducks. There are pairs, king pairs and Audis.

More rarely, we have the fool's golden duck. This is where a scorecard shows a batter being dismissed for 0 (1). However, the batter wasn't dismissed first ball (the true golden duck). Instead, the batter survived that delivery, only to be run out from the non-striker's end before facing another. Excellent stuff.

And, obviously, when it comes to being run out from the non-striker's end, we also have the diamond duck. That's where a batter is dismissed for zero, having faced no deliveries. It's a batting performance of complete and perfect emptiness – the *Transformers* sequel of knocks. The finest example of the diamond duck remains, of course, Allan Donald's superb, doomed dash for the match-winning run in the 1999 World Cup semi-final.

This match remains the greatest one-day international of all time. This is despite the best efforts of England and New Zealand two decades later, tying the World Cup final. But the nod must go, by the barest of margins, to the 1999 semi-final.

That tipping point nod can be credited to Donald and batting partner Lance Klusener. The heroics of Klusener to pull South Africa to the brink of victory, followed by the absurd run-out that undid it all, is a story climax that cannot be topped. It's both the funniest tragedy and the darkest comedy. A piece of drama surpassing anything scripted.

The image of a futile, batless Donald being overtaken by Damien Fleming's underarmed roll to Adam Gilchrist for the run-out is iconic. One that will never be forgotten by anybody who saw it. A duck for the ages.

Yet topping this and all other ducks is the most legendary duck of them all. The one we discussed at the beginning of this section. The one scored by Bradman, when he only needed four runs in his final Test innings to ensure he retired with an average of 100.

Yes, cricket has not one, but two widely acclaimed Donald ducks. And if that kind of effortless Disney one-upmanship isn't yet another reason to cement cricket as the greatest sport in the world – the dux of sports, if you will – then I don't know what is.

NEXT:

Ducks are funny, but they're not the only thing about cricket that is. Let's talk about the comedy of cricket. Plus, pioneering knock-knock joke writers!

THE COMEDY OF CRICKET

PETER WHO?

IS SELECTED FOR A TEST

Selectors

THE MOMENT:

With England having secured the Ashes in Melbourne in the 1986 Boxing Day Test, the Australian selectors start 1987 by picking unknown off-spinner Peter Taylor for the fifth Test

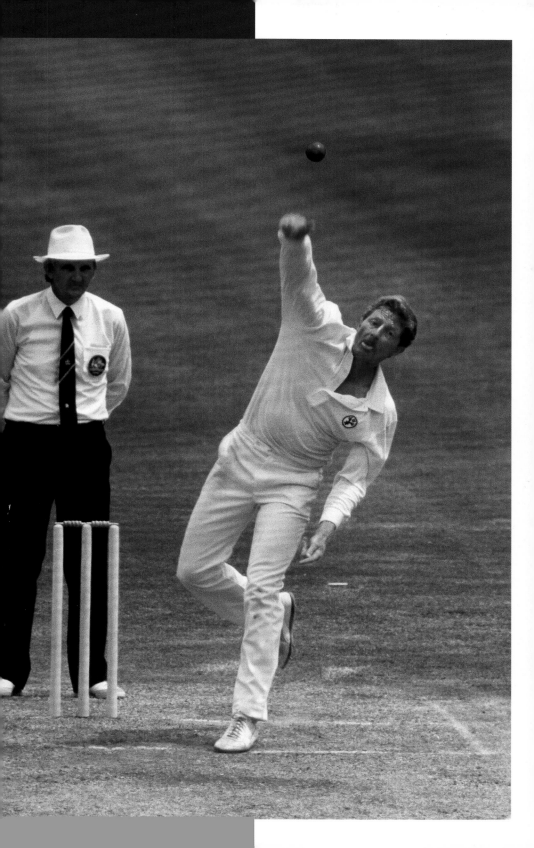

Selectors are unlikely sources of comedy. To an outside observer, their role might seem a simple one: choose the best possible team from all the candidates. In a sport as numbers-based as cricket, that might seem a trivial task. Something that could be handed over to a well-designed spreadsheet.

But spreadsheets aren't funny. (Notable exception: a numerical analysis of all the *Police Academy* films. Oh, Tackleberry! The hilarity of your gun-toting excessive police brutality will never go out of date.)

Which is why human selectors still have a role.

In good times, there aren't many opportunities for selectors to wield their comic wares. Meg Lanning's current Australian women's side need only fifteen seconds of CTRL-C'ing and CTRL-V'ing. Then perhaps a chicken parma and several beers, before everybody wobbles their way home, job well done. Steve Waugh's and Ricky Ponting's respective teams presumably required similarly trivial clipboard and pub work.

Oh, sure, sometimes Trevor Hohns would get it into his head that he needed to plan for the future. He'd then mix things up by making plans to get rid of beloved legendary players. Telling Steve Waugh that he'd been axed as captain of the ODI side during the Allan Border Medal is decent shock comedy, I guess.

However, it's when the national team is foundering that selectors have the best opportunity to flex their comic muscles.

They can work on running gags. For example, the repeated selection of Shaun and Mitch Marsh based on brilliant domestic form. Followed by the inevitable axing of Shaun and Mitch Marsh based on international form that proved, yet again, to be less than brilliant.

They can then riff on that bit with the selection of some other Mitches, including both Johnson and Starc. Set up a Mitch- and Marsh-centric team foundation so that, in 2014, it was possible to break down the Australian team as follows:

Mitches: 3

Marshes: 2

Mitch Marshes: 1

Non-Mitch Marshes: 1

Mitch Non-Marshes: 2

Non-Mitch Non-Marshes: 7

Non-(Mitch Marshes): 10

In tough times for the ODI team, selectors with a keen eye on the humour of the situation can choose players based on BBL form. A hypothesis that domestic T20 form translates to international 50-over success is worth exploring. For comedy potential if nothing else. One might even dub this 'The Big Bash Theory' of selection, if one were interested in piggybacking on the inexplicable success of the nerd sitcom of a similar name. Bazinga!

If the captain of the side is struggling, a solid piece of comedy is to stick by them. Especially when any non-comedic analysis of their form would see them axed. This was a policy most flagrantly enacted for Mark Taylor, circa 1997. However, it was also employed with Aaron Finch during the lead-up to the 2019 World Cup. (A period where captain Finch would only have been the first player selected if such decisions were based on first-name alphabetical order.)

Or you can pick a player out of nowhere. Just to mess with people. That comedic bit worked with Ashton Agar in 2013. It worked – by necessity – with about two-thirds of the Australian Cricket Board team during the World Series Cricket period in the 1970s.

And it worked like absolute crazy with the selection of Peter Taylor in 1987.

If selectors have their greatest comic opportunities during periods when the team is terrible, then the 1980s offered potential not seen since pioneering knock-knock joke writers first set foot in the town of Nantucket.

On their 1986/87 tour of Australia, England had retained the Ashes with no trouble at all. They'd also dominated the early rounds of the annual ODI tri-series (and would go on to win it). They'd also won the Benson & Hedges Challenge, a bizarre four-team tournament to celebrate the, uh, America's Cup yacht race?

Australian cricket had been pummelled all summer by England. So with one Test remaining, selecting Taylor was a last-gasp attempt to salvage something – comedically, at least – from the series.

The headlines following his selection read 'Peter Who?'. As if he were a shock candidate to be the next Doctor. So obscure was Taylor that many fans have speculated over the years that his selection was a mistake. That the selectors had meant to choose the previously mentioned *Mark* Taylor. Mark was at least an up-and-coming young opener at the time. Peter was just a lookalike for Principal Ed Rooney in *Ferris Bueller's Day Off*. He was more likely to be selected for a celebrity impersonation gig at the post-Ashes ball than as an actual off-spinning member of the team.

The 'they meant to select Mark' speculation formed the basis of cricketing conspiracy theories for decades. Another wonderful comedic touch from the men choosing the team.

And the comedy didn't end there. Because Taylor went on to vindicate the selectors on a *cricketing* level. They'd pulled a joke rabbit from the hat. But the rabbit turned out to be a jumpy off-spinner with a spring in his bowling step, a windmill in his action and a debut player-of-the-match performance in his heart.

Australia won the toss and chose to bat. Taylor made his first impact on the match late on the first day, with his side at 7/232, joining Dean Jones, who had backboned the innings with a stoic century. Taylor added 11 in a partnership of 39 with Jones. It was part of a fine wagging of the tail that saw Australia recover from 5/184 to 343 all out.

Then Taylor was given the ball. Merv Hughes and Bruce Reid had dislodged England's top three of Chris Broad, Bill Athey and Mike Gatting to have the visitors at 3/17. Unfazed by the step up in level, Taylor worked his way through the rest. Flighting the ball, he had the batters falling to uncharacteristically-sharp-for-1980s-Australia catches close in. Then finished off the tail with a couple of deliveries that turned sharply between slogging bat and firmly planted pad.

Taylor finished with 6/78 from 26 overs, to give Australia a 68-run lead on the first innings. Then, to ram home his worth as a cricketer, he again contributed to a solid partnership in the second innings. Coming in at 7/145, he combined with Steve Waugh. Taylor added 42 in a 98-run partnership to help Australia set England a target of 320 runs.

Taylor took two wickets in the second innings – Allan Lamb and Ian Botham both for the second time. His fellow spinning Peter, Peter Sleep, took 5/72 – including the final wicket of the match, with only one over remaining in the day, to give Australia victory by 55 runs. But Taylor's startling debut won the bulk of the accolades, including the official accolade as player of the match.

The selectors may have delivered an outstanding piece of comedy with his selection. But Taylor had provided the perfect punchline.

NEXT:

Selectors stumbling into good decisions is funny. Cricketers strutting into terrible ones is funnier. Plus, meme-worthy explanations!

DEAN JONES

ASKS CURTLY AMBROSE TO REMOVE HIS SWEATBANDS

Collapses

THE MOMENT:

In the first final of the 1992/93 ODI tri-series, Dean Jones asks West Indies fast bowler Curtly Ambrose to remove his wristbands, triggering a series of furious bowling spells that saw Australia repeatedly collapse

If you're familiar with Twitter and/or rating systems and/or dogs, then you're probably aware of the WeRateDogs (@dog_rates) account. As the handle suggests, it's a Twitter feed consisting of pictures of cute dogs. Each photo is accompanied by a brief summary of the canine in question and a rating out of, yet invariably exceeding, ten.

Of course, being Twitter, it was only a matter of time before somebody took umbrage at this. The umbrage thief in this case was a hero named Brant. His sensible objection was that 'you give every dog 11s and 12s'. A complaint countered with the illogical but immediately meme-worthy explanation: 'they're good dogs Brent'.

It's easy to be on the side of Brant (aka Brent) here. Such freewheeling disregard for the very foundations of maxima needs to be stamped out. But then one remembers batting collapses, and all logical principles are discarded.

Because there are many different kinds of batting collapse. And they're all amazing. Each and every one of them deserves to score at least 11/10. Fidelity to mathematical axioms be damned.

The purest breed of batting collapse is the one that begins early and ends early. It's the 36 or 47 or 51 or 58 or 60 or 67 all out, where nobody gets started. Instead, the batters turnstile their way to and from the middle until the innings is put out of its misery.

A flawed team effort from top to tail, the perfection of the sub-100 total batting collapse is easy to understand. A century is considered an admirable, yet attainable, target for an individual batter. For an entire team to fail to reach that goal is a display of such great disdain for the art of batting that it has to be admired. This kind of collapse is therefore the 'best in show' of collapses. It's the batting collapse against which all others are measured. 13/10.

But there are other kinds of batting collapses, of all shapes and sizes. Collapse-lovers around the cricketing world take enormous delight in identifying and classifying the various types.

Consider, for example, the batting collapse that comes from nowhere. A team's top order is coasting along, establishing a half-decent total. Their fans begin to contemplate the prospect of something massive.

Then, a wicket.

And another.

One more.

And before the team knows it, they're all out. Those previous extrapolations that seemed so justifiable are instead recast as the height of foolish optimism. This is a standard schadenfreude breed of collapse. One for lovers of subverted expectations everywhere. 11/10.

The reverse of this, where a team's top order are swiftly herded away from the middle, back through the gates to the dressing room, is a good, solid, working-class collapse. A bit of top-order folly that's saved by a late recovery. A rescued collapse is a special kind of collapse, and nothing puts a smile on the face of cricket fans quite like a happily wagging tail. Who's a good collapse, then? 12/10.

But it's not just *when* the collapse happens that defines it. There are other factors that batting collapse aficionados learn to look out for.

Sometimes, for example, batting collapses emerge due to the pressure of the match situation. A team sees a win on the horizon, and reacts with an unfettered choke. These choker specials are an especially reliable breed of batting collapse. They're popular throughout the entire world, from Cape Town to Johannesburg and everywhere in between. 13/10.

Another, rarer variation is the elongated batting collapse. Most batting collapses happen fast. They feed on dressing-room panic as the next batters in scurry to get their kit together. In contrast, a long collapse is an unusual breed. One that arises in the specific

case of a team batting so defensively, in an attempt to ensure a draw, that they forget to score runs. The finest of these absurd-to-behold, elongated batting collapses came during the Adelaide Ashes Test in December 2006. The mere idea of an extended collapse in which, over the better part of two sessions, nine wickets were lost for 60 runs, costing a team the Ashes, is a splendid one. 12/10.

Other times, collapses arise from a terrifying spell by a particular fast bowler. It might be Donald terror. Or Jofra terror. Or a great moustachioed Mitchell terror. Whichever it is, the relentlessness of this breed of collapse makes it irresistible. And perhaps no kind of terror was harder to resist than pure Ambrose terror.

Curtly Ambrose was one of the greatest fast bowlers in the history of the game. He was more than two metres tall. This height allowed him to extract vicious bounce from a good length. At speeds of around 150 kilometres per hour.

Why Dean Jones decided to antagonise him remains a source of bafflement to this day.

It was during the first final of the tri-series in 1992/93. As was so often the case, it was Australia against the West Indies. The West Indies, batting first, had made a middling 8/239.

When Australia began their chase, Richie Richardson gave Ian Bishop and, mysteriously, Phil Simmons the new ball. This was enough to annoy Ambrose. Irked, he took the wicket of David Boon, which brought Dean Jones to the crease.

Jones immediately asked Ambrose to remove his sweat bands. The Australian number three insisted at the time that the white material made the similarly white ball too hard to see. Jones would later claim it was a tactical ploy to try to put Ambrose off his game.

It did not work. Ambrose bowled heat, taking 5/32 to give the West Indies victory. (Although, not just heat – a key wicket was an exquisite slower ball that left Ian Healy baffled and bowled.)

Nor was that the end of it. Ambrose took 3/26 in the second final. Then he put in back-to-back player-of-the-match performances in the fourth and fifth Tests as the West Indies fought back from 0–1 down to win the series 2–1.

In the fifth Test, at the WACA, the series was on the line. Australia were disappointed, then, to fall from 2/85 to 119 all out in their first innings. Ambrose finished with 7/25 from 18 overs. His seven wickets came in a spell of five and a bit overs. It cost one run and effectively secured the series

for his side. A pure Ambrose terror collapse. 12/10.

It's impossible to choose a favourite collapse from among the countless breeds. Especially if you include the wide variety of mixed-breed batting collapses. Collapses that combine the various strands of comic DNA found in the purer versions. Have you ever seen a Broad-faced Duke's ball swinger's special? It's the cutest thing imaginable. 60/10.

But regardless of whether they're purebred or mixed, batter- or bowler-inspired, long-tailed or short-tailed, the best thing about collapses is that whatever type you end up with, you know you're guaranteed a piece of comedy cricket you can rely on. A fan's best friend.

They're all good batting collapses, Brent.

NEXT:

More hilariously terrible decisions from cricketers. A closer look at South Africa's World Cup woes. Plus, Mandela effects!

MARK BOUCHER
PLAYS A DOT BALL

South Africa Choking

THE MOMENT:

Needing to beat Sri Lanka in their final game to qualify for the Super Six stage of the 2003 World Cup, hosts South Africa misread the Duckworth–Lewis sheet and instead dot out the final ball

Mel Brooks once said: 'Tragedy is when I cut my finger. Comedy is when you fall into an open sewer and die.'

When it comes to cricketing sewer-falling death, there is no grander running gag than South Africa's ongoing 'crashing out of World Cups' routine.

From the moment South Africa returned to international cricket in 1992, they staked out their comedic terrain of 'heart-breaking World Cup exits'. They have defended it heroically ever since. Within this limited field of humour expertise, the comedic virtuosi of South Africa contrive to weave fresh humour. All they need to showcase their hilarity are a few raw ingredients: ties, rain and semi-finals. Those three elements can be mixed and matched in ever-changing ways.

In 1992, their last-minute inclusion in the tournament was a curiosity. Cricket fans at the time vaguely knew of the concept that South Africa played cricket. Tales had been told of Barry Richardses and assorted Pollocks. Plus, every now and then, a heap of a Test nation's fringe and/or over-the-hill players would head over there on a 'rebel tour'. It was all a little bit naughty and alluring.

But now South Africa had returned for real. There was a whole new international cricket team to play against. From out of nowhere. The best possible kind of Mandela effect. And South Africa were *good*. Good enough to make a World Cup semi-final on their first attempt. Only to be undone by rain. And, of course, by the rain rule that saw their target move from 22 off 13 balls, to 22 off seven and, finally, laughably, 22 off one ball.

In 1996, South Africa were an even better cricket side than they'd been in 1992. They blitzed the group stage. They beat the United Arab Emirates by 169 runs. Then New Zealand by five wickets with 75 balls to spare. England they beat by 78 runs. Pakistan by five wickets with 34 balls to spare. Finally, they crushed the Netherlands by 160 runs.

As top-of-the-table finishers in Group B, they earned the right to face the lowest-ranked qualifier from Group A in a quarter-final. That lowest-ranked team was the West Indies. The West Indies were a once-great side in decline, with only a few of their legendary players remaining.

Ah, but one of those remaining legendary players was Brian Lara, at the absolute peak of his powers. Lara peeled off a century at better than a run a ball to knock South Africa out of the tournament. It wasn't a semi-final exit, but for comedy purposes it was close enough.

In 1999, South Africa and Australia tied their semi-final. Australia went through to the decider based on their better record in the earlier rounds. A decent game. You may have heard people talk about it.

Which brings us to 2003, a World Cup South Africa hosted and were expected to dominate. Or, at the very least, to co-dominate, along with the very unfunny, never-losing Australian team of the era.

Instead, South Africa struggled. They soon found themselves needing to beat Sri Lanka in their final game merely to qualify for the Super Six stage. Chasing 269 for victory off 50 overs, South Africa stumbled to 5/149 in the 30th over. Wicketkeeper Mark Boucher and captain Shaun Pollock led a fightback. Then the rain began to fall, increasing in heaviness throughout the 45th over. With two balls remaining before the umpires would surely take the players off, Boucher coolly smashed a six to reach the Duckworth–Lewis par score.

But rather than try to score the match-winning run off the last ball of the over, Boucher blocked it to midwicket and refused the single.

Brilliantly, inexplicably, hilariously, the South Africans had read the Duckworth–Lewis sheet wrong. They'd mistaken the match-*tying* total

for a match-*winning* one. And that tie saw them exit the World Cup.

It was the peak of South Africa's comedy cricket. Of the three weapons in their World Cup slapstick arsenal – ties, semi-finals and rain – the ties and the rain were the big guns. The semi-finals were mere icing on the cake. (Assuming you can have a cake made out of guns. I wouldn't know. I'm not American.)

Since that 2003 peak, South Africa have cruised, laugh-wise. In 2007 they made the semi-finals again, where they chose to collapse to 5/27. Despite a partial recovery to reach 149, Australia ran down the total with seven wickets and 111 balls remaining. Which was fine – there's nothing wrong with a good collapse, as we've seen – but it did not quite capture the magic of earlier tournaments.

In 2011 and 2015, South Africa were knocked out by New Zealand. First, in a quarter-final, again after topping the group stage. Then the second time in an epic semi-final, in which Grant Elliott (born and raised in South Africa, so perhaps a comedic plant?) hit a match-winning six with two balls remaining.

In 2019, they didn't even bother to make the knockout matches.

Which is a shame. Because outside of their World Cup exits, the South

Africans aren't a particularly funny bunch. They're boring, methodical, robotic cricket machines. They tend to drop out of the comedy cricket scene in non–World Cup years. One assumes they use the time off to develop their regular quadrennialish show. Like some kind of cricketing Cirque du Soleil. (Except, y'know, entertaining.)

So let's hope that when 2023 rolls around, they'll be back at their hilarious best. Ideally ticking all the boxes as they tie a semi-final while rain falls all around them. Maybe they can even lure Brian Lara out of retirement to inflict a masterclass upon them. For old times' sake.

But also because, without South Africa's little World Cup exit skits, there's a very real risk that somebody might someday take a closer look at Australia's Test record. If they ever do, they might realise which nation should truly own the 'choker' tag.

For any serious examination of tight Test match defeats reveals that Australia occupy a disproportionate share of spots. Of eleven Tests lost by ten runs or fewer, Australia have lost six of them. (They've won three, all of which took place in 1902 or earlier.) And of the fourteen losses by one wicket, Australia claim another six (with just the one victory, in 1951).

Australia have not won a tight Test match in *seventy years*. Ouch! That's exactly the kind of cricketing finger cut that somebody might ridicule, if South Africa ever stop falling down open sewers.

NEXT:

Cricket fans may have treated South Africa unfairly. But unfairness is built into the sport's very fabric. Plus, car rental customer service attendants!

GLENN MCGRATH
SCORES A FIFTY

Tail-end Batting

THE MOMENT:

In the first Test against New Zealand in 2004/05, Glenn McGrath scores his only Test fifty, making 61

There are certain people who claim that cricket is a batter's game. These liars, to call them by their correct name, ignore one very obvious fact. Hardworking batters are at almost all times forced to face the best bowlers the opposition can muster. This is in stark contrast to those easy-living bowlers. They're regularly given the opportunity to bowl to people with batting techniques well below the best available.

I refer, of course, to tailenders, whose very existence is yet another reason why cricket is the greatest sport in the world. Because, as with peacocks, tuxedoes or sperm, when it comes to batting orders, it's the presence of a tail that elevates the unremarkable into something special. Something that, to varying degrees of literalness, makes life worth living.

The first great gift of tailenders is their identifiability. Tail-end batters offer a relatability unmatched in any other sport. For many fans, much of the joy of watching elite sport is the thrill of watching human beings (plus whatever beautiful breed of alien creature AB de Villiers is) stretch the very limits of the contest's requisite skills as they engage in the fiercest of competition. And, to be sure, cricket offers that. It might be Bradman vs Larwood. Or Richards vs Lillee. Or Kohli vs

Cummins. Or any other combination of elite batter confronted with elite bowler you'd care to name.

But multiple times in every match, cricket offers something different. The challenge of elite batter against elite bowlers gives way to a much less even contest. The same bowlers who were before tangling with batters on the same plane as them are now faced with opponents nowhere near that plane. The equivalent of baggage handlers, perhaps. Or car rental customer service attendants. Or the staff who help the elderly and dim-witted wrangle the automatic check-in terminals.

And as we head further and further into the aeronautical fringes of this admittedly strained batting metaphor, fans of the game are given a glimpse of what it might be like if we, the non-elite, cricket-watching amateurs, were permitted to enter the contest.

None of us can realistically envision what it must be like to bat with the skill of, say, Kane Williamson. But we can watch Chris Martin and imagine ourselves filling his inept shoes. Flailing our bat for a handful of deliveries until we are outclassed by an international-standard bowler.

Because, in most cases, the mismatch does end swiftly. As you'd hope. After all, if a batter's innings doesn't correlate to some degree with their batting ability, then we're playing something akin to dice cricket. And that's no fun for anybody. (Yes, I went there. Come at me, Big Cricket Simulation Gaming.)

But the correlation of the progression of a batter's innings to their batting prowess isn't perfect. Bradman, after all, didn't score 99.94 every time he went out to bat. In fact, he never once made that score, the old fraud. There's a natural variability to batting performances.

Which means that sometimes, if we're very lucky, the tailender can transcend their limitations. Sometimes, they manage to compete with a bowler who would generally swat them away with minimal effort. And that's when tail-end batting becomes more than relatable. It becomes funny – the second great gift of tailenders.

We've all seen instances of a pair of tailenders shrugging their shoulders, deciding to have a bit of a tonk and then implausibly getting away with it. And there are few things more delightful to watch.

Ricky Ponting captained one of the most dominant teams in Test match history. Right up until the point that he didn't. And yet, amid that success, including a run of sixteen consecutive victories, the moment that seemed to bring the most unbridled joy to him and his team was the 114-run partnership between Jason Gillespie and Glenn McGrath against New Zealand in 2004.

Three years earlier, New Zealand had arrived in Australia and held Steve Waugh's all-conquering home side to a 0–0 drawn series. If they were hoping to emulate that feat on the 2004 tour against Ponting's all-conquering side, that hope dissipated by the third day of the series.

The first two days hadn't been bad for New Zealand. Captain Stephen Fleming won the toss and his side made 353. But Australia wiped out the deficit shortly after lunch on the third day, five wickets down. A mini-collapse then saw the home side stumble from 5/438 to 9/471.

But that ninth wicket brought Gillespie and McGrath together. And the pair then added a preposterous 114 for the tenth wicket. Gillespie finished with 54 not out and McGrath 61. (The pair then took five wickets between them as New Zealand collapsed for 76. A less than ideal twenty-four hours for the Black Caps.)

Only one thing would have made McGrath's Test half-century more entertaining. That would have been if he'd somehow been able to take the runs off his own bowling. McGrath the bowler would have been enraged by McGrath the batter's antics.

Because the other great thing about tail-end partnerships is how furious they make the opposition. And the better the bowler, the more likely they are to be infuriated by their counterparts having the temerity to treat them in such a fashion. And the angrier the fielding side gets, the funnier it is for everybody watching.

This is true no matter when it happens. If the top order has collapsed and the tail rescues the innings with their tomfoolery, that's funny. But if the fielding team has taken forever to pry out the proper batters, only for the tail to extend the torture, that's funny too.

However, as great as it is to see two tailenders having a thrash, there's one combination that's even better. The specific combination of a tailender and a genuine batter provides the third great gift of tailenders. A sporting battle of wits between established batter and fielding captain. A contest where all tactical choices lead to dynamite entertainment.

The fielding team can allow the batter the single to give the tailender the strike, only for the batter to deny it. This has the potential for hilarious run-out panic at the end of each over.

The fielding team can choose not to alter their field. The batter might then manipulate the strike to put on a large final-wicket partnership. All while the inept tailender barely faces a ball. That's maddeningly delicious stuff too.

A batter taking the single the fielding team offers, and then the tailender slogging it everywhere? Yep, that's magnificent.

The worst-case scenario is the batter giving the tailender the strike, only for them to be immediately dismissed. But even that at least gives us the schadenfreude of a frustrated not-out batter second-guessing themselves as they trot off the ground.

This is a win-win-win-win game theory matrix, where the winners are the spectators. And it's yet another demonstration of why the batting weaknesses of tailenders and everything associated with them remain one of cricket's greatest strengths.

NEXT:

The success of an inept batter is ripe comedic turf. The success of a great batter requires something more special. Plus, never-ending children's ditties!

GREG CHAPPELL

BREAKS BRADMAN'S RECORD

Overthrows

THE MOMENT:

In his final Test innings, in January 1984, Greg Chappell surpasses Australia's record Test runs tally, held by Don Bradman, thanks to overthrows

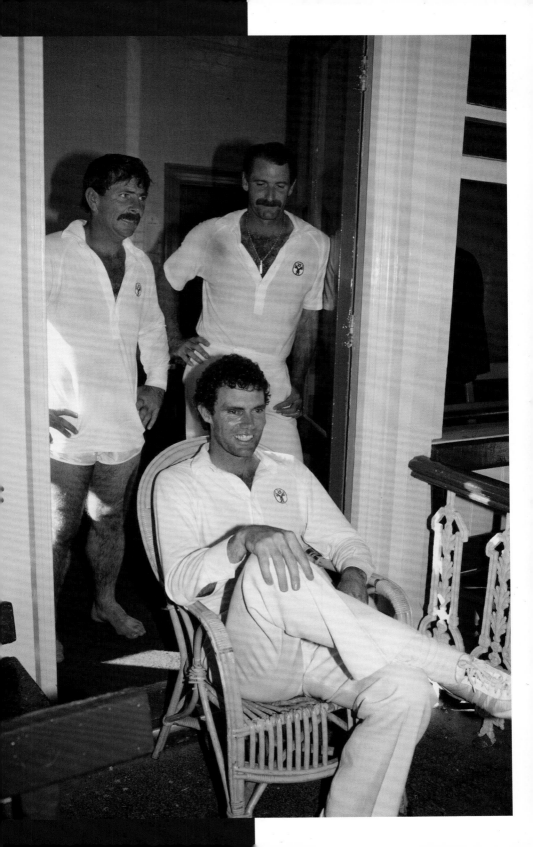

Greg Chappell's retirement announcement came during the fifth Test against Pakistan in 1983/84. At the time, he was on 6928 career runs in Test cricket. That left him 68 short of the Australian record of 6996, held by Don Bradman.

Chappell claimed he was unconcerned by the record. 'If you're playing for records then you shouldn't be playing,' he told the media. 'Catches and runs are not that important.'

Still, he had that day equalled Colin Cowdrey's record for most Test catches, after pouching Mudassar Nazar. And 68 runs wasn't *that* far away for a batter of Chappell's skill.

He received a standing ovation all the way to the middle, coming in at number four. To the surprise of nobody, he then went on to make 182 in his final innings. The ton made him only the third player to score a century in both his first and final Tests.

But the key moment was the breaking of Bradman's record. When Chappell was on 65, three runs short of the Don's tally, he defended the ball into the covers and called Kim Hughes through for a single.

The cover fielder, Mohsin Khan, flew in, picked up the ball and flung it at the stumps at the non-striker's end. Chappell was safely home. But no fielder was backing up, and the ball flew away towards the boundary for overthrows. As fielders set off in pursuit, Hughes and Chappell scampered through for three bonus runs – the runs that made Chappell the most prolific scorer in Australian Test match cricket.

Now, ordinarily, it'd be annoying as all get-out that Chappell brought up the record with four runs, three of which came from overthrows.

Not the overthrows bit. No problem with that. But the four part of it.

Generally speaking, an overthrow that doesn't end at the boundary lacks a proper denouement. Without the climax of the ball crossing the rope, the joy of the misfielding lacks a satisfying payoff. Much like flashback-based sitcom *How I Met Your Mother* or children's ditty 'The Song That Doesn't End'.

Furthermore, overthrows that result in a final total of four or six runs are less satisfying. This is due to their similarity to standard boundary scores. Yes, there is some joy to be had in the moment from these overthrows. But they will usually soon be forgotten. Lost forever in the historical cricket statistics databases alongside such humdrum everyday shots as a cover-driven four or a Glenn Maxwell switch-hit six while falling over with his eyes closed.

The most notable of recent overthrown sixes is the Ben Stokes deflection in the final hysteria-induced panic attacks of the 2019 World Cup final. But it should, as every know-it-all has poindextered out by now, *technically* have been a five.

This would have been fitting. Because from any particular delivery, the greatest run tally that can be taken from it is five. Not the greatest in magnitude, of course: there are literally countless numbers greater than five. That, after all, is how the Peano axioms of arithmetic were designed. But five *is* the greatest run tally in terms of comic enjoyment, a far more important aspect to the seasoned cricket fan.

There is something glorious about a five in cricket. Any delivery that sees five added to the score has been a delivery in which something very special indeed has occurred. (And I'm not even including penalty runs due to the ball hitting the wicketkeeper's helmet.)

It is, of course, possible that the five has been all run. The pair of batters scurrying back and forth between the wickets like trapped lemmings in the computer game *Lemmings*, *Lemmings 2: The Tribes* and *Lemmings 3: Tokyo Drift*. But this is unlikely. The haste required from any batting pair in pursuit of an all-run five would usually inspire a corresponding urgency in the fielder in their corresponding pursuit of the ball. Given such fielding urgency, even the most insatiable of batters tend to settle for the almost-as-glory-laden all-run four.

No, the most likely source of a five is the overthrow that transforms a hurried single into something five times more valuable. The overthrow five is a Hero's Journey of a delivery. The call to an adventurous single. The crossing of the threshold into a dangerous world where there is a realistic chance of a run-out. The ordeal of the ball being flung at the stumps. Before, finally, the triumphant reward of the ball beating the backing-up fielder and going all the way to the boundary.

The overthrow five is the Platonic ideal of an overthrow, superior to all other forms.

It's better than an overthrow for seven. A seven has other clear merits. It's critical in subverting the entire concept of the ludicrous usage of 'maximum' as a synonym for a six, for example. However, a seven is less likely than the overthrown five to be the result of a genuine run-out opportunity. An overthrown seven is more likely to be a frustrated fielder realising that the batters are running a three and pinging in a relay throw that goes astray. Which is fine. But it's less comic than the purity of the five overthrows and so loses points in comparison.

And don't get me started on overthrow eights. An all-run four followed by four overthrows? That's a hat on a hat, people. Comic gluttony. Get a grip.

No, the five is the most satisfying tally of runs to be scored from any given delivery. A reliable source of cricketing comedy, infuriating bowlers and captains since time immemorial.

So, yes, a five would have been a fitting way for Chappell to break the Don's record. Simply because fives are the best.

But we can make an exception in this instance. Bradman's final run tally was four short of giving him an average of 100, all thanks to a comic shortfall of runs in his final innings. It therefore seems fitting that Chappell would go past Bradman's record in *his* final innings thanks to a four, reached via a comic *excess* of runs. That's a neat circle, perfectly closed by an imperfect piece of fielding.

Thirty-four years later, Alastair Cook, England's most prolific Test run scorer, brought up a century in *his* final innings. Like Chappell, the final Test century paired with a debut ton. But Cook's century was achieved thanks to an overthrown five.

And that's why he's now Sir Alastair Cook and Greg Chappell

remains sadly knighthoodless. Some of us may allow the overthrown four in specific circumstances. But the Queen? She's a stickler for the comic perfection of the overthrown five.

NEXT:

Wayward releases of the ball aren't limited to fielders. Ladies and gentlemen, I present to you Mr Stephen Harmison. Plus, third-party lawsuits!

STEVE HARMISON

HARMISON

BOWLS A WIDE

The Ashes

THE MOMENT:

With England looking to defend the urn in the 2006/07 Ashes, Steve Harmison sends the first ball of the series wide to first slip

The 2005 Ashes series was among the greatest Test series ever played. One of the best teams the game has ever seen (plus Shaun Tait) went to England, where they met a home team finally willing to go toe to toe with them. Over five Tests, the challengers refused to back down against the champion Australian team. They recovered from 1–0 down (and the brink of 2–0 down) to win back the Ashes 2–1. The result was only secured on the final day of the series, following a heroic 158 from Kevin Pietersen.

The series reignited cricket in England. All the England players were awarded MBEs for their Mighty Batting/Bowling Efforts (delete as appropriate). Passion for cricket in England following the 2005 Ashes reached new heights. So much so that it remains a constant source of bafflement as to why England haven't since chosen to go another sixteen years without winning the Ashes. Perhaps they've tried, and the cunning Australians have outwitted them. In which case, excellent work, Michael Clarke and co.

So, when the England side returned to Australian shores eighteen months later to defend the urn, excitement for the series could not have been higher. The 2006/07 Ashes was the most anticipated Test series in decades. Everybody in world cricket, but particularly England and Australia, were riveted. Desperate to see what these two teams would do when they finally met again.

The intensity derived not from a simple one-off series. For the ecstasy of England's 2005 victory was not just due to those two months of cricket. It derived instead from a decade and a half of torment.

Australia had regained the Ashes in 1989 in a completely surprising 4–0 victory on English soil. Throughout the 1990s, Australia continued to dunk on England at every opportunity. They grew stronger and stronger, adding more and more champion players to their team, until it became faintly ridiculous. England, by contrast, seemed to get worse and worse. They couldn't match Australia for quality of players. But they surpassed them in quantity. England's selectors turned over prospect after prospect. All in a doomed bid to find even a few parts of a team that might hope someday to get close to thinking about competing to some extent in an Ashes series.

It never worked. Even when the scorelines seemed close, they weren't. Anybody who watched the 1997 Ashes, for example, can confirm that England were somehow thrashed by a margin of 3–2.

From 1989 to 2002/03, England were clowned every single time they even pretended to compete for the Ashes. No wonder 2005 was so satisfying for them. No wonder it was so devastating for Australia.

And heck, it wasn't only the previous fifteen years that had laid the groundwork for the 2006/07 series. It was the entire history of the Ashes, one of the most celebrated sporting trophies in existence.

The idea of the Ashes was first coined in a mock obituary in 1882. It was later realised in physical form by the burning of a bail. Since then, Australia and England have scrapped for the tiny urn that represents cricketing supremacy between the two nations. (Even if England never *actually* hand it over, no matter how large the thrashing.)

It's a contest taken seriously by players and fans from both countries. A rivalry so intense that it tends to swamp all other series in which the nations compete. Australia or England might take part in matches against objectively worthier opponents. But even so, one eye will always remain on the next Ashes series, whenever that might be.

From an objective point of view, that's ridiculous. But that's okay. The Ashes *are* ridiculous, a fact often forgotten because of how seriously everybody involved takes them.

But we shouldn't forget that the Ashes started as a joke. No matter how much hype and anticipation surrounds any given series, there should always be some element of absurdity.

Which is why, in an environment of unprecedented anticipation, excitement and hope for another great Ashes series, Steve Harmison's first ball made for such a perfect moment of comedy.

In the 2005 series, Harmison had set the tone. In the first session of the first Test, after Australia won the toss and elected to bat, it was Harmison who bounced Australian captain Ricky Ponting. It was Harmison who cut Ponting's cheek with a ball that smashed into the grille of his helmet, literally drawing first blood in the contest. It was Harmison who led the fiery England attack, taking 5/43 as they blasted Australia out on the first day for a mere 190.

Comedy is about the subversion of expectations. Great comedians are able to lead their audiences down a seemingly predictable path, only for that path to collapse, producing an unexpected outcome (for example, a third-party lawsuit over path maintenance standards) that, ideally, elicits laughter.

Harmison had the entirety of Ashes history to help him with the setup to the joke. But the punchline was all his.

With all eyes on the most talked about first ball in a Test series ever, umpire Steve Bucknor called 'play'. Harmison, a giant at the top of his mark, glistening under the Brisbane sun, charged in to bowl. Facing him was Justin Langer, squinting up at Harmison and tapping his bat in readiness. The fans in the crowd – Australian and Barmy alike – roared and clapped with excitement. The noise built in volume with each stride Harmison took.

As the crowd's whistling and hollering reached its peak, Harmison reached Bucknor. He took the final leap of his run-up, his right arm whipping over, straight and tall, as he delivered the ball.

The ball flew down the pitch. Then off it. Well wide of Langer. Well wide of the keeper, Geraint Jones. But unwide of captain Andrew Flintoff at first slip. Flintoff took the wayward delivery with the confident air of a car-wash attendant being tossed the keys to a four-wheel drive that's never set wheel outside the city limits.

This is no problem at all, was the air that Flintoff attempted to exude. *Everything is under control.*

But everything wasn't under control for England.

The tension that had built up over the years, the decades, the full 120 years of Ashes cricket, dissipated. As one, the Gabba laughed.

And England? As in 2005, they allowed Harmison to set the tone. They backed up his strong first-ball comedy instincts by losing the 2006/07 Ashes series 5–0. Not even the hilarious England joke sides of the 1990s had managed that. In retrospect, an even better justification for all those MBEs.

NEXT:

Bonus moment! We come full circle. Plus, shenanigans suspicions!

(REPRISE). SHANE WARNE BOWLS MIKE GATTING

Reactions

THE MOMENT:

After Shane Warne bowls him with the
ball of the century, Mike Gatting reacts

Shane Warne bowling Mike Gatting encapsulates everything that's great about cricket.

It highlighted the skill of Warne. As we've already discussed in some detail, way back at the beginning of this book, Gatting was dismissed by one of the single greatest exhibitions of skill the sport had seen.

The dismissal also highlighted the laws of the game. Gatting had attempted to nullify Warne's Ball of the Century by using his pads. The ball had pitched outside leg stump, so if Gatting had been able to get any part of his substantial body in line with the ball's trajectory, he would not have been given out.

Gatting's failure to pad the ball away was due to how far the ball spun. So far, in fact, that his initial reaction betrayed a suspicion that there had been a Spirit of Cricket violation. Was he actually out? Or was Ian Healy shenaniganing up a wicket-cheating storm?

The delivery also showcased the evolution that Warne brought to the Australian side. Leg-spin had been seen before, of course. But it was out of fashion. And leg-spin à la Warne truly *was* something new. Enormous spin? With pinpoint precision? Nobody had ever bowled like this before. Australia had dominated the previous two Ashes campaigns without Warne. With him, they would skyrocket to an unassailable level.

Allan Border's deployment of Warne also highlighted the Australian captain's tactics. He'd told Warne to bowl within himself in early tour matches. In a warm-up against Worcestershire, Graeme Hick had smashed Warne around, scoring 187 as Warne took 1/122 off 23 overs. Border needed to reassure his leg-spinner. 'It doesn't matter,' he told him. 'This is just about you getting some rhythm. Him thinking you can't bowl works in our favour, show him nothing.'

Then there are the numbers, always a fundamental aspect of cricket. There would be plenty of numbers going forward, even if we limit our examination of them to Warne's appearances against England. An astonishing 195 Test wickets, the most by any bowler against a single country. Of those, 129 *in* England, at an average of 21.94. More than 10,000 balls bowled to England batters. And this delivery was number one. In every sense.

Which, finally, brings us to comedy. And Gatting's showcase of reactions to the dismissal. Warne would make fools of plenty of people over the next thirteen or so years of his career, not least himself. But Gatting will always be his most famous fool (despite the best efforts of Daryll Cullinan). Not just for the fact that he was dismissed by the Ball of the Century. But because his reaction to the dismissal was so perfectly befuddled and comical.

The cameras at the ground captured the immediate aftermath. Gatting looking back at the stumps. Trying to work out what on earth just happened. Then the raised eyebrows of surprise as he removed his gloves and began to come to terms with the fact that he'd somehow been bowled.

In the commentary box, Richie Benaud clarified the visuals for viewers still trying to come to terms with what they'd seen.

'Gatting has *absolutely no idea* what has happened to it,' said Benaud.

And it was so obviously true. Gatting looked as if somebody took the image search results for 'quizzical confusion', morphed them all into one and then superimposed it back onto his face.

'He *still* doesn't know,' Benaud added.

Almost three decades later, it's possible Gatting may still not know what happened.

But we know. Warne had showcased cricket at its very best, with every element of the sport coming together in a moment of sublime perfection.

Absolute gem of a sport. The best there is.

MORE TITLES FROM DAN LIEBKE

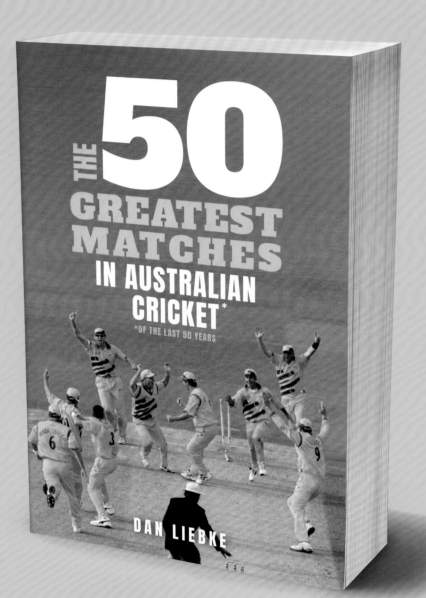

THE 50 GREATEST MATCHES

IN AUSTRALIAN CRICKET*

*OF THE LAST 50 YEARS

DAN LIEBKE

The 50 Greatest Matches in Australian Cricket

What makes a cricket match truly great? Is it broken records or heroic defences? Tight victories or humiliating defeats? A classic sledge that sticks in the mind? Or is it those incredible stories and monumental moments that make some contests live on forever?

Matthew Hayden scoring 380 against Zimbabwe might qualify for the record books, but not for this book: these are the Tests, ODIs and T20 matches that transcend the numbers and will be talked about long after the participants have hung up their pads.

Relive the breathtaking ties, impossible chases, and even the devastating losses that created cricket legends as we count down to the greatest match with sports journalist and cricket tragic Dan Liebke. An essential collection of cricketing tales for any fan of our national sport.

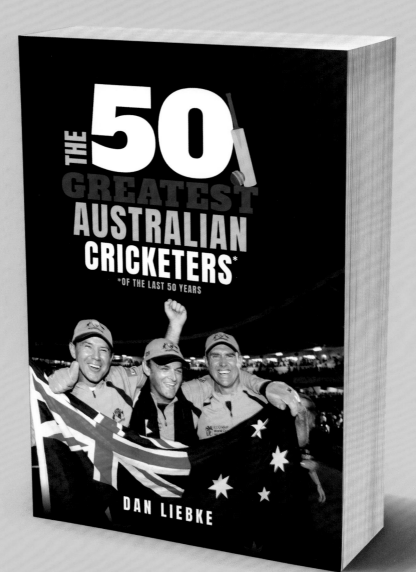

THE 50 GREATEST AUSTRALIAN CRICKETERS*

*OF THE LAST 50 YEARS

DAN LIEBKE

The 50 Greatest
Australian Cricketers

Some are born great, some achieve greatness, and some have greatness thrust upon them by virtue of their skills with ball and bat. This book is about the latter.

Australia's favourite sport has a proud history of turning nobodies into somebodies and ordinary men and women into heroes of international renown.

From the black-and-white belligerence of Ian Chappell to the colourful celebrity of Shane Warne, the diplomacy of Adam Gilchrist to the ruthlessness of Meg Lanning, the pantheon of Australia's greatest cricketers is as mottled as the crowds that cheer them on. But who is the greatest of them all?

In *The 50 Greatest Australian Cricketers*, sports journalist and comedy writer Dan Liebke charts the careers, characteristics and enduring legacies of the finest Australian cricket players of the past 50 years.

IMAGE CREDITS